THE BIG BOOK OF NEVADA GHOST STORIES

THE

BIG BOOK

OF

NEVADA

GHOST STORIES

JANICE OBERDING

Globe
Pequot

Essex, Connecticut

Globe
Pequot

An imprint of Globe Pequot, the trade division of
The Rowman & Littlefield Publishing Group, Inc.
4501 Forbes Blvd., Ste. 200
Lanham, MD 20706
www.rowman.com

Distributed by NATIONAL BOOK NETWORK

British Library Cataloguing in Publication Information available

Library of Congress Cataloging-in-Publication Data

Names: Oberding, Janice, author.
Title: The big book of Nevada ghost stories / Janice Oberding.
Description: Essex, Connecticut : Globe Pequot, [2023] | Includes
  bibliographical references. | Summary: "Time has all but forgotten the
  tragic tales of those who have passed through Nevada, but their spirits
  remain. As arguably the most haunted state in the nation, Nevada has
  more than its share of ghosts with intriguing stories and historical
  connections. Among them is the unfortunate gangster, Bugsy Siegel who
  died in Beverly Hills only to return to his old stomping grounds, the
  Flamingo Las Vegas; Julia Bulette, the ill-fated prostitute who was
  slaughtered in her bed on a cold January morning in 1867; and the many
  haunted houses in Reno, their owners forever tied to their homes,
  refusing to depart"—Provided by publisher.
Identifiers: LCCN 2023004944 (print) | LCCN 2023004945 (ebook) | ISBN
  9781493073467 (trade paperback) | ISBN 9781493073474 (epub)
Subjects: LCSH: Ghosts—Nevada. | Haunted places—Nevada. | Ghost
  stories.
Classification: LCC BF1472.U6 O2347 2023 (print) | LCC BF1472.U6
  (ebook) | DDC 133.109793—dc23/eng/20230501
LC record available at https://lccn.loc.gov/2023004944
LC ebook record available at https://lccn.loc.gov/2023004945

In loving memory of Bryan H. Smalley,
my Goldfield friend who rocked the world with
his love and knowledge of Central Nevada,
its minerals, its gems, and its history.

Contents

Reno

Lake Tahoe Area

Washoe Valley, Genoa, Carson City, and the Carson Valley

Central Nevada

Eastern Nevada

Southern Nevada

Introduction

I am proud to call Nevada home. There is no other state quite like the Silver State, which might never have been if not for that silver. Silver was discovered near Virginia City in 1859, and soon the world was paying attention to this drab little place called Nevada. Luckily, Abraham Lincoln needed Nevada and its silver to turn the tide and win the Civil War and the presidential election.

In what is the longest telegram ever, telegrapher James Gould worked seven hours sending the entire (16,543-word) Nevada Constitution to Washington, DC, so that Congress could vote on Nevada's statehood. In the deal, the US government would claim ownership of more than 84 percent of Nevada's land, the highest percentage of any state. Nevadans still don't like this. It is apropos that a state with so many ghosts was admitted to the union on Halloween, October 31, 1864.

Forty years after attaining statehood, Nevada's future looked bleak. Its silver had been depleted, and with no other resources to offer, Nevada stood to lose statehood and be swallowed up by other states. Sacre bleu! This would not have been a good thing. Those strong men and women who came westward and put roots down here would have been rolling in their graves if they hadn't already been haunting various locations throughout the state.

Thank goodness for Tonopah's Jim Butler and his burro, who discovered a new vein of silver in Central Nevada as the twentieth century dawned. Wealth and new citizens for the state were assured by word of Butler's find. Before the twentieth century concluded, the state's abundance would be found 250 miles south of Tonopah in the city of Las Vegas, which incidentally wasn't even part of the state of Nevada on October 31, 1864.

That's a brief history. Now for those ghosts and their stories. As one of the most racially diverse states in the United States, Nevada has a rich culture, and that includes stories about ghosts. Nevada has more than its share of ghosts. Some have argued that Nevada is one of the most haunted states in the nation. That may or may not be true. But one thing is certain. Nevada's ghosts are certainly intriguing. Among them are nameless men and women that time has all but forgotten—save for their occasional ghostly appearances. Then, too, there is the unfortunate gangster Bugsy Siegel, who died in Beverly Hills, only to return to haunt his old stomping grounds, the Flamingo Las Vegas; and Julia Bulette, the ill-fated Virginia City prostitute who was slaughtered in her bed on a cold January morning in 1867. Nevada's oldest ghosts are the ancient Anasazi people, who simply vanished thousands of years ago. Some of them have remained to haunt the area where they once lived.

Before we begin our journey into the Silver State's ghosts, I'll remind you that in 1931 Arizona's then governor G. W. P. Hunt called Nevada a "ghost state." I'm sure he meant that in a derogatory sort of way, but Nevada governor Fred Balzar was quick to respond. He invited Hunt to visit Nevada, where he would find some of the liveliest ghosts imaginable.

I agree with that sentiment. Not only are Nevada's ghosts lively; they are as varied as a Nevada sunset. Let's take a look.

Northern Nevada

Virginia City

It's a small town. Nonetheless, Virginia City happens to be Nevada's most haunted city. So it's only fitting that we begin our quest for ghosts here in this little town on Mount Davidson. Virginia City abounds with ghosts and their stories. There are those who will tell you that Virginia City is, without question, the most haunted city in the United States—yes, even ahead of New Orleans, Salem, and Gettysburg. It's a possibility if you're counting ghosts per square mile.

Long before the Cartwrights rode into nighttime television, Virginia City made its mark. And with apologies to those purely fictional Cartwrights, there were more miners, by far, than cowboys and ranchers living in Virginia City. This was because of the silver and the opportunity it afforded to become an overnight millionaire—if one were very lucky.

Silver! With its discovery the world came rushing up Sun Mountain (later Mount Davidson) and founded this cosmopolitan town.

From its beginning, Virginia City's population was diverse. And so was the food. The Mexicans brought their culinary skills, as did the Cornish, the Chinese, the Italians, the Irish, the African Americans, the Germans, the Scots, and the Native Americans. Tastes were as varied as the people who eked out a living here on the hill.

Along with those existing on very little were the millionaires who made their fortunes in mining. Sandy Bowers and John Mackay are but two who made the quick ascension from miner to millionaire. Bowers died young, leaving his widow, Eilley, to struggle with creditors and critics in a world that was very much *a man's world*. John Mackay fared better. His name is everywhere at the University of Nevada campus, including Mackay Stadium, where the wolf pack trounces (or so it is hoped) all comers. Mackay's family made all this possible with the generous sums they gave to the university. The Mackay Mansion where John Mackay once lived is one of Virginia City's treasures—complete with ghosts.

Mackay Mansion

*A*lva Gould and Abraham Curry founded the Gould and Curry Mining Company in 1859. The building we know today as Mackay Mansion was built a year later to serve as the mining company's office and the home of its mining superintendent.

The first superintendent to live in the building was George Hearst (father of newspaper magnate William Randolph Hearst), who made the family fortune in mining in Utah, South Dakota, and Montana—he may not have struck it rich here in Virginia City, but his dream of wealth surely began here when he purchased interest in the Gould and Curry Mine and the Ophir Mine.

Now, you are no doubt wondering how this building came to be known as the Mackay Mansion. That's because John Mackay lived here, albeit ever so briefly. And he would not have lived here at all if not for the Great Fire of 1875 that destroyed 75 percent of the city and left more than three thousand people homeless. Among them was John Mackay, whose mansion on A Street was devoured in the raging flames.

With his wife and family living abroad in Paris, Mackay moved into the empty home of the Gould and Curry Mining superintendent. Some may argue that Louise Mackay moved into the mansion with her husband, but Mrs. Mackay was not fond of Virginia City, and most historians tend to disagree. Yes, I know that there have been many ghost investigations at the mansion in which Louise Mackay has appeared. She has her own reasons for doing so, and whatever they may be, she is not alone here. An elderly man and a ghostly little girl also haunt the mansion. Actor Johnny Depp may have encountered her.

It was 1995, and Johnny Depp was in Virginia City. The locals were thrilled to have a movie star in their midst. By all reports, Depp visited with many of them in the local saloons and was warm and friendly. He was here working on his current film *Dead Man*, a western that was filmed entirely in black and white. When the subject of ghosts came up, someone suggested that Johnny stay at the Mackay Mansion—it was haunted and everyone in town knew so.

The story is that while staying at the Mackay Mansion, Depp encountered the ghost of the little girl in the doll room. Of course, if you're going to verify the authenticity of a story, you've got to do a little research. So I did. It turns out the February 1995 issue of the magazine *Premier* carried the interview with Depp in which he discusses, among many other things, ghost hunting at the Mackay Mansion. So there it was—verification that Johnny Depp saw the ghostly little girl at Mackay Mansion.

Elvira and Howard Kiehlbauch, the parents of my late friend Theresa Behnken, owned the Mackay Mansion from 1962 to 1988. Years ago, I asked Theresa about some of the Mackay stories I'd heard. The ghostly army colonel and the young girl were two I was most curious about. Theresa told me that she and her mom had encountered the paranormal, particularly the little girl, an old man, and a young man. I was curious who they might have been.

"Lyman shot himself in what they call the Gold Room," Theresa said solemnly. "I believe he is the old man that haunts the place."

She had no information other than his name, so I set out to find more about the man she called Lyman. Could he have been D. B. Lyman, mining superintendent in Virginia City, I wondered. If so, I could find plenty about his life, but nothing on how it might have ended. My research would happen months after this conversation. And on this day, Theresa wanted to talk about her time at Mackay Mansion and the ghosts she encountered.

"The last little girl to live in Mackay Mansion was Mary Ruth Douglass Nicholson," Theresa informed me. "She was born in 1896, the only child of Julia Agnes Keeley Douglass and William Gilbert Douglass. He was the Nevada secretary of state from 1903 to 1911. He made a fortune in mining, so I'm sure Mary Ruth wanted for nothing."

"Do you think she is the little-girl ghost?" I asked.

"I don't know—she was eighty-four when she died in 1980. I guess she could be," Theresa replied. "Some of the dolls and such that were here might have belonged to her."

Theresa was quick to explain that she didn't feel fearful of any of the Mackay Mansion ghosts. No one did. In fact, in an earlier day, sometime in 1962, a séance was conducted in the kitchen at the Mackay Mansion. Theresa's mother, Elvira Hermann Kiehlbauch, was descended from a long line of fortune-tellers, psychics, and mediums and felt that it was important to communicate with the resident ghosts.

"Mr. Douglass had a reputation of sorts. They say he ran away, leaving a girl pregnant in Illinois, and never sent a penny to help her or her son," Theresa said. "We called for him first. As soon as we said his name we heard a thud and a loud moan. Then it sounded like something was crawling across the floor, and then something materialized—that's when we turned the lights on. We weren't afraid," she said. "But afterwards my mother worried that we might have opened a doorway that night. There was one negative ghost that came into my bedroom sometimes, and he was very frightening—it was almost as if he enjoyed scaring me."

Several years ago a group of friends and I decided to do our own séance at the Mackay Mansion. It was mid-March, but I must tell you that I've never in my life been as cold as I was that night sitting at the table in the Mackay dining room. An inch or two of snow was on the ground, and the owner, for whatever reason, refused to turn on the heat or light the fireplace. It went as séances generally do until my friend Kristin Hamlet had her long red hair pulled by an unseen hand. From that moment, the activity became overwhelming. The ghostly little girl appeared to several people at the table. Those who didn't see her clearly heard her crying.

At that point my husband, Bill, appeared to lose interest in the séance. Some at the table believed he had been possessed, claiming that his voice and face had actually changed. He of course denies this and puts it down to overactive imaginations at work. But clearly the ghostly residents wanted to make their presences known.

A Night at the Clampers'

*T*he E Clampus Vitus is a men's fraternal organization that was founded in West Virginia by Ephraim Bee sometime in the mid-1800s. There are several chapters throughout the west; our story concerns the Juliette C. Bulette chapter in Virginia City.

The only way to become a member of the E Clampus Vitus (Clampers) is to be sponsored by another member. And the sponsor's name remains secret forever—a member must never divulge his sponsor's identity under any circumstances. That's for men; women are not permitted to join the E Clampus Vitus, although they are considered to be members (widders) if their significant other is a member.

No one but a Clamper is permitted to spend time in their building in Virginia City, except during open house. I'm usually doing something else on these rare occasions when they open up the building to the public. So I told myself that chances were I'd never see the inside of that building. That changed recently when I took part in Con-Con 5, which is an annual paranormal event held in Virginia City.

Do I have to tell you how thrilled I was when I found that the location where I would be leading groups in ghost hunting for the night was the Clampers' building? The Clampers are keen on local history. In efforts to make sure that no historic place, or person, is ever forgotten, they place plaques at sites that have played an important part in Comstock history. Thus, the history of this area is preserved.

Jason Virden, aka the Mayor, greeted the group at the staircase and led us upstairs to the room where the Clampers gather. As you'd expect, there's a bar with comfy barstools, well cushioned and old. Historic photographs and other memorabilia line the walls. What caught my eye was the line of vests that hung from the ceiling. Jason explained that vests are important. When a *brother* passes on, his vest is hung here forever, provided his widder or family can bear to part with it.

I suggested that the ghosts here might not be so happy that women were here doing some ghost investigating. Jason put my doubts to rest. He then told us about the ghostly activity Twin Paranormal got on a visit here last year. And so we began. Some of the best evidence came from those who are psychic sensitives. One woman got the name of a recently deceased brother. Since she lives out of state, it is doubtful she could have known this. Another person did a psychometry reading on the hat of a long-dead brother. According to Jason, she was spot on.

For the investigation, some investigators were using what is known as a spirit or ghost box. This is a popular piece of ghost-hunting equipment that continuously scans through radio frequencies creating white noise, which allows a spirit to communicate with (speak to) the living.

During a quick spirit box session, a man in the group asked how he could become a member of the Clampers.

The reply was, "Talk to us."

When it was my turn to ask a question, I decided to have a little fun with the ghosts.

"So tell me, how do I become a member of the Clampers?" I asked.

The reply was of the four-letter variety, and I won't repeat it here. Suffice it to say that whoever was speaking with us from the great beyond clearly did not appreciate my effrontery or my question.

For Whom Did the Bell Toll?

*T*he Delta Saloon is said to house a very haunted object with the Suicide Table. Legend has it that the old faro table was the site of several deaths that took place near it. Several owners of the table have died by their own hand since Black Jake lost his life savings of $70,000 one night at the table. After his death, Black Jake was thought to still be hanging around. Even to this day, his apparition, dressed in black from head to toe, makes an occasional appearance at the Suicide Table.

Black Jake is believed to be the angry man former employees say they've encountered in the kitchen. Step out of his way. Otherwise, he will walk right through you, leaving you chilled to the bone.

A mystery at the Delta involves the old haunted call bell. A call bell, for those who aren't familiar, was mounted on the wall near the gaming table and was used to summon the bartender with drinks when a player was thirsty. On March 31, 1873, the *Gold Hill Daily News* reported that on Saturday morning, March 29, during a faro game at the Adriatic Saloon a few doors down C Street, players were startled to hear the call bell start ringing. No one was near the bell, and certainly no one had rung it—probably just a fluke, or maybe the ground was shaking, they assured themselves, and kept playing. Later the same night, the call bell at the Delta Saloon began to ring of its own volition. Those at the table watched as the bell slowly rang without the aid of anything or anyone earthly.

Because there were no wires and there was no way the bell should be ringing on its own, those present were convinced a ghost was at work. One player was so frightened he got up and left the saloon. A dealer was said to have panicked but continued dealing the game. Later the names of two recently deceased patrons of the Delta were suggested as the ghostly bell ringer.

And although word spread and other newspapers picked up the story of the *ghost bell*, there was never any evidence as to who the ghostly culprit was. The call bell is long gone at the Delta Saloon, but the ghosts are said to remain. But not to worry. Except for Black Jake, they are very friendly.

Ghost at the Writer's House

*W*alter Van Tilburg Clark was one of Nevada's most distinguished writers. In 1988, Clark, the author of two literary classics, *City of Trembling Leaves* and *The Ox-Bow Incident*, received the posthumous honor of being the first inductee into the Nevada Writers Hall of Fame. During the last years of his life, he served as a writer in residence at the University of Nevada–Reno and edited the *Journals of Alfred Doten*. He made his home in Virginia City. And that house is still standing; there are no plaques, and most visitors to town aren't aware of its literary significance or of the ghost stories about the house.

During Clark's residence, the sitting room featured floor-to-ceiling bookcases. Virginia City tales claim that one of those who moved into the house shortly after the writer's death complained of weird noises, like books being tossed around near the bookcases. Needless to say, this person didn't stay long. Then there was the shadowy figure standing at a front window that frightened another person away.

"Everyone knows that place is haunted," A Virginia City friend told me when I asked her about the ghost story. "People moved in and moved out in a big hurry. I don't know—they said it was the ghost."

"Do you think the ghost might be Walter Van Tilburg Clark himself?" I asked. Now that would be a story—authors caught in the act of haunting former residences.

She took a sip of her drink and dashed my hopes. "I don't know. Could be anybody. Walter Van Tilburg Clark wasn't the first person to live in that house."

Walter Van Tilburg Clark died in 1971 at the age of sixty-two and is buried at the Silver Terrace Cemetery in Virginia City. And it's my guess that he's still there in his former home, making plans to read every book he had in his library.

Jack Sheppard's Dog

*J*ack was a nervous old yellow dog when his owner Judge A. W. Baldwin died in a California train accident in 1869. Jack waited—and waited. But when the judge didn't return to Virginia City, the hungry dog began wandering the streets. Surely he could find something to eat and someplace to stay. He ended up in the Gold Hill dog pound, suddenly facing a grim future. If someone didn't come and claim him soon, Jack would be shot; thankfully, the canine wasn't aware of this.

And then Jack Sheppard showed up. Sheppard was a miner who happened to be in the market for a dog. And Jack caught his eye. Sheppard made his choice, paid the fee, and took the dog. For the next three years, the nervous old yellow dog and the miner were inseparable. The only problem was the old dog was squeamish about noises. Gunshots or other unexpected loud noises caused him to howl loudly and incessantly.

Jack Sheppard didn't mind, for he loved his dog, idiosyncrasies and all. Then came the day when a loud blast at one of the mines startled the dog so badly that he dropped dead of a heart attack in front of the Vesey House. Jack Sheppard was heartbroken. He'd always feared this day would come, but he hoped it would be years down the road. In his sorrow, he scooped up his beloved old companion and buried him near the Kentuck Mine.

But there were those at the Vesey House who swore that every night at midnight, a loud mournful howl rose up from the ravine and echoed across the canyon like a steam whistle. Jack Sheppard's dog, they said—and although he was dead, the dog was not yet ready to be silenced.

Today the Gold Hill Hotel is the former Vesey House. If you should be in the vicinity late at night and hear what sounds like a dog howling in the distance, don't be alarmed. It's only Jack Sheppard's dog.

Lucius Beebe at the Cemetery

*O*penly gay in a less enlightened time, Lucius Beebe and his partner, Charles Clegg, are said to be responsible for helping to bring Virginia City back from the decay it had fallen into after the Great Depression when the mines had stopped producing. Lucius Beebe was a wealthy, well-known bon vivant, gourmand, writer, and train historian. Author of more than thirty-five books, Lucius Beebe was inducted posthumously into the Nevada Writers Hall of Fame in 1992.

Photographer and writer Charles Clegg coauthored many of Beebe's books on trains and train history. Tired of big-city life, the two men moved from New York to Virginia City in 1950. Here they purchased the *Territorial Enterprise* newspaper, famous for having been the newspaper where Samuel Clemens got his writing start and where he took the pen name Mark Twain.

Beebe and Clegg settled in a historic house and began socializing with other Virginia City writers and artists. They were enjoying new friends and the good life in their little town—and then *Bonanza* came to television. It was 1961, and suddenly there were tourists. They were driving up the winding Geiger Grade for a glimpse of where the Cartwrights might have walked. Never mind that the Cartwrights were the creation of television scriptwriters, people kept coming by the carloads, disturbing the once peaceful little town.

Virginia City was no longer the haven that Beebe and Clegg had fallen in love with. They sold their house and most of their belongings, packed up, and moved to San Francisco. They would live there until Lucius Beebe died of a heart attack in 1966 at the age of sixty-three. In 1979, Charles Clegg tragically died by suicide at the same age Beebe had been when he died.

Somewhere around this time, the stories began. The ghostly Lucius Beebe, always the snappy dresser, began appearing in elegant evening attire at the Silver Terrace Cemetery gates, looking forlornly toward the east. Was he looking for Charles Clegg or reminiscing about the good times they'd shared so many years ago in Virginia City? To my knowledge, no one has ever asked him that question.

The Ghost Who Was Here and Gone

*T*his was one of those ghost stories that began in the summer of 1876 and was all but forgotten with the first snowstorm. The ghost made its first appearance in the northeastern section of Virginia City just as the sun was going down. The ghostly glowing figure spread its arms a moment and vanished as quickly as it had appeared. Many of those who witnessed the apparition believed it was that of a recent murder victim.

Still others held a different opinion as to the ghost's identity altogether. The glowing sundown specter, they insisted, must be one of the unfortunate Grosch brothers, the first discoverers of the Comstock Lode. Surely if anyone had a right to be angry at the way their lives had ended, it was the Grosch brothers. They had found it all. But fate had cruelly decreed that neither Hosea Grosch nor his brother Ethan Allen would live to enjoy their discovery. Now one of the Grosch brothers had returned to the Comstock, angry at it all.

There were plenty of arguments about the ghost in the saloons and in the mines. But winter came, and all was forgotten. The ghost, for whatever reason, made no further appearances.

Ghost on a School Bus

Riding the school bus is an adventure that's been enjoyed by schoolchildren for decades. Of all the places a ghost might haunt, you wouldn't think that a school bus would be very high on the list. But there is the ghostly little boy that bus drivers discuss in hushed tones. They've seen him but aren't sure what to make of him. He rides the school bus through Virginia City and out toward the Mark Twain area.

He is dark-haired and neatly dressed, and like most little boys, he can be mischievous. He enjoys pranks like hiding bus drivers' keys and other items when he is in a playful mood. Apparently the little ghost appears to the drivers but not to the school bus passengers. That's probably just as well. None of the bus drivers who've seen him have a clue as to who he might have been. This doesn't stop the ghostly little boy from boarding the bus and going on a ride-along.

Mark Twain on the Boardwalk

Then away out in the woods I heard that kind of
a sound that a ghost makes when it wants to tell
about something that's on its mind and can't make
itself understood, and so can't rest easy in its grave,
and has to go about that way every night grieving.
—Mark Twain, Huckleberry Finn

Samuel Clemens came to Virginia City in 1862 and began his
illustrious writing career on the *Territorial Enterprise* newspaper
using the pen name Mark Twain. He only stayed in Virginia City until
1864, when he was forced to leave town after challenging an editor
to a duel. Dueling had been outlawed and Twain found himself on
the wrong side of the law, so he fled to California.

He returned to the Comstock only once more during his lifetime;
this was to give a lecture on the Sandwich Islands at Piper's Opera
House and to cover the execution of Julia Bulette's killer, John Millian, for a Chicago newspaper.

However, a longtime Virginia City story has the ghostly Mark
Twain sauntering up and down the boardwalk in the wee hours of
the morning. He never speaks, and in fact those who've seen him
say he appears to be agitated and not in the best of moods. This
could be just another tall tale, but then again more than one person
has sworn off drinking after encountering the specter.

The Faceless Woman of A Street

*T*his story has been told for decades in Virginia City. In *Meet Virginia City's Ghosts*, an early ghost book about Virginia City, author Marge Reboton shared the story of the faceless woman who haunts A Street. I'm not going to lie to you. In some of my early ghost-hunting forays, I wandered up to this spot on A Street in hopes of an encounter with her. I met a couple of friendly dogs and skeptical wild horses, but the faceless lady ghost was elusive. Perhaps this ghost story is based on the boarder at Crazy Kate Shea's lodging house who in October 1876 got drunk, knocked over an oil lamp, and started the most devastating fire to ever sweep through Virginia City.

Or she may be Crazy Kate herself. The ghost of the faceless woman is always seen in the vicinity of Crazy Kate's old boarding house. And if she isn't screaming in terror, she's crying. Just how she does this without benefit of a face is beyond me, but that's what those who claim to have encountered her will tell you. If she is Crazy Kate, she's donned a modern wardrobe in comparison to what she wore in the nineteenth century. The faceless woman is wearing slacks.

And she is menacing. No one has ever been harmed by the faceless woman, but then no one has ever enjoyed the encounter either, especially those who witnessed her appearance at the old Presbyterian Church on C Street. She stepped into the church and looked around (again, how she managed this without a face will be left up to your imagination). Satisfied, the ghostly woman then turned and walked out the door.

Crying Baby at the Silver Dollar

*F*lorence Ballou Edwards, who owned the Silver Dollar Hotel from the 1940s to the 1960s, was a colorful and eccentric woman who enjoyed chocolates and gossip. According to Virginia City lore, she allowed late-night guests to take a key from a cigar box on the desk and select their own room; the next day they could register and pay for their room. The Silver Dollar was not the most upscale place, but guests were generally assured a good night's rest. That is, until the baby began to cry—and cry.

Guests often wondered why the mother wasn't more attentive to the baby that cried incessantly throughout the hotel. "There is no baby," Edwards explained to disgruntled guests. But their ears told them differently. One night some guests went from room to room conducting their own search for the crying baby. They found that Edwards had told them the truth. There was no baby on the premises, so where were the cries coming from?

Virginia City is haunted—that's a given. Eventually people accepted the fact that the baby just might be another ghost. Infant mortality rates were high in the nineteenth century. Perhaps the long-ago baby died nearby and rests at the Silver Terrace Cemetery. And for whatever reason, the ghostly baby sometimes wails its displeasure for any and all to hear.

The Ghost Who Hated Christmas

*V*irginia City is a place you either love or you don't. Those who love it find a way to live here one way or the other. Such was the young couple who bought their first house, a tiny one-bedroom cottage, during the Thanksgiving holiday season. Years ago, they shared their story of living with what is referred to as an anniversary ghost; the ghost only made itself known at one specific time of year. In this case the ghost came at Christmastime.

It was their first Christmas in their first home. In a rush to celebrate the season, they decorated their little cottage ahead of everyone else. When they were finished, they agreed that their house looked beautiful—like an old-fashioned picture postcard of the Comstock, with the outdoor lights reflecting on the snow. But the ghost didn't like all the holiday jolliness.

On Monday morning the couple went back to work, and the ghost set about unscrewing the Christmas tree bulbs from their sockets. The tinsel and ornaments were left in a pile on the parlor floor. Their first thought when they returned that evening was that someone had broken into their house. But no windows were broken, and no locks had been tampered with. Nothing was missing. Except for the Christmas lights, tinsel, and ornaments, everything was just as they had left it. A cold night, they turned up the heat and put the lights back on. That's when all the power went out.

The husband checked the fuse box and found that it was blown. A quick repair, but the Christmas tree lights were ruined. No matter how many strings of lights they put up, the fuse box was blown and the lights were ruined. They decided to do it the old-fashioned way and decorated their tree with lots of icicles and no lights. As they sat on the sofa admiring their tree, it toppled with a thud.

The cat was playing with the tree, they thought. But when they found the cat curled up on the bed, they decided there was something else at work here—a ghost!

"Okay! We get it. You don't like Christmas. But we do. So please just do us a favor and leave the tree alone," the husband said. "And," he added playfully, "don't open the presents."

The ghost must have heard him. The presents were not disturbed, and the tree was only occasionally touched. Once Christmas was over and the tree and decorations were taken down and put away, things went back to normal. This didn't stop the couple from selling the house and moving out before the next Christmas came to the Comstock.

Does Katherine Hillyer Haunt the Spite House?

A spite house is not unique to Nevada. Many locations across the county have their own spite house and stories. In Virginia City the spite house includes a ghost or two. For those who might be asking just what a spite house is, I'll explain. It is just what the name implies: a house built out of spite, usually very near the house of the person who is spited.

The story in Virginia City is that sometime between the late 1940s and early 1950s, a miner built himself a house with windows on all sides. But his longtime enemy couldn't bear the thought of the miner enjoying his light and airy home.

What could he do to make the miner miserable? Finally he came up with a solution: He built a house on the property line, which was about twelve inches from the miner's home, thus making all windows on that side of his house worthless.

Later in the 1950s, two well-known Nevada writers, Katherine Best and Katherine Hillyer, bought the spite house. Known locally as the two Katies, Best and Hillyer loved their home and didn't seem to mind the spitefulness. Aside from a ghostly little dog, Katy Hillyer is thought by some to haunt the house to this day. Not everyone agrees that Hillyer is the ghost there. According to some, she haunts the Delta Saloon, where she and Katherine Best spent many happy hours drinking and partying with their old pals and fellow writers, Lucius Beebe and Charles Clegg. There is also the story about her ghost being seen on the C Street boardwalk as the inveterate reader races toward the bookmobile, her arms full of books.

I can see a ghost getting around and haunting more than one location. Former owners told of items being moved around and of disembodied laughter that can be heard throughout the house. Maybe it was one of the two Kates, and maybe it wasn't.

Since there have been no ghostly appearances, the identity of the ghost can't be determined—other than the dog.

The Red Camel

In the southwest United States, many stories are told of the ghostly Red Camel. Here in Virginia City, Mexican miners first told of *el camello fantasmal* (the ghostly camel) that appears on full-moon nights and makes its way across the canyons and over the top of Mount Davidson. The camel's passenger is always a grinning skeleton.

Camels came to Nevada by way of the US Army, which imported dromedary (one-hump) camels to haul materials in 1836. Many years later, Bactrian (two-hump) camels were brought to Nevada for hauling supplies across the desert and up to Virginia City. Camels were not well received in Virginia City. No one liked the creatures they considered strange looking. They were unfriendly and ugly, and besides that, they frightened horses.

Camels had other problems as well. Unlike horses with strong hooves, camels have soft pads and were not suited to Nevada's rugged terrain. In order to solve the problem, Virginia City passed an ordinance banning camels from its streets during daylight hours. The Nevada legislature went even further by passing a bill that outlawed camels from all public roads. By that time, camel owners realized the animals were just too much trouble. They cruelly set the animals free to roam the hostile desert. The lucky ones perished quickly. Others wandered aimlessly through the canyons near Virginia City for years afterward.

This may have been the beginning of Virginia City's legend of the Red Camel. If you should ever see the ghostly Red Camel, you will never forget it. Sitting atop the beast is a grinning skeleton that guides the camel through the terrain around Virginia City.

Ghosts on Parade

*T*he Virginia City RV Park near the Silver Terrace Cemetery is a popular spot with visitors to Virginia City who want to enjoy modern convenience camping. Many years ago, a friend of mine got more than modern convenience when she vacationed at the park.

I'd just fallen asleep when my two dogs started to bark. No matter how much I yelled at them, they kept barking and barking. I love my dogs, but they were driving me crazy. Wide awake now, I sat up, pulled the curtain back, and looked out the RV's back window to see what had them in such an uproar. I didn't see anything.

By now the dogs were up in my face, barking to beat the band. "Be quiet!" I scolded them, and looked out the window again.

Off in the distance was a group of people who were solemnly walking across the cemetery. No living person glows like that; they had to be ghosts. And I was scared. I didn't want the dogs to call attention to us—for all I knew, the ghosts would come to the motor home and haunt us.

Crazy thoughts like that raced through my mind. I opened a bag of treats to keep the dogs quiet and watched what seemed like a parade procession. What on earth are they doing? I wondered. Why are they following each other? I didn't have time to think about that. As I stared at them, the ghosts began to vanish, one after the other, until they had all disappeared.

I turned on all the lights, wrapped up in my old bathrobe, and didn't sleep another wink for the rest of the night.

Lavinia

Death is but a kindly frost that cracks the shell and
leaves the kernel room to germinate.
—Headstone of Lavinia W. Lannen

*T*hose in Virginia City could hardly ignore Spiritualism as it swept
across the country. This new religion, brought about by the spirit
communication of the Fox sisters in Hydesville, New York, was especially embraced by women. Spiritualism offered women the opportunity to publicly stand on equal footing with men for the first time
ever. Indeed, many of the famous women Spiritualists, who lectured
in Virginia City, also became involved in the early women's movement of the suffragettes.

In Virginia City, as elsewhere across the country, Spiritualism
societies were formed so that like-minded people could gather to
socialize and communicate with the dead. Housewife Lavinia Lannen conducted séances at her home, helping people to speak with
their dearly departed. Highly regarded for her ability to work with
the dead, Lavinia must have truly enjoyed her work and has decided
to stay on. She is said to walk the area near her grave at Silver Terrace Cemetery to this very day—and night.

Fourth Ward School

*W*hen it opened its doors to students in 1876, the Fourth Ward School was considered the utmost in schools with its indoor heating and plumbing. In its October 15, 1876, issue, the *Daily Territorial Enterprise* said the following of the school:

> The pride of Virginia is the new school-house which is going up on the Divide. If it is our pride today, the time is not far distant when it will be our glory as well.

In 1936, the last class was graduated at the Fourth Ward School, and the school would stand empty until 1986, when the Fourth Ward School Museum was opened to the public. Today it continues as a museum and a place where exciting Virginia City cultural events take place.

The oldest legend here at the Fourth Ward School is the ghostly Miss Suzette, aka the hitchhiker, a teacher who waits outside the old school. This ghostly young woman is said to appear on rainy nights only after darkness overtakes the Comstock. Over the years, a few unsuspecting motorists have stopped for her, thinking she needs a ride into town or down the hill.

Unlike some hitchhiking ghosts, Miss Suzette doesn't get into the car. Instead, she smiles warmly and vanishes before a driver's startled eyes. Miss Suzette, they say, was killed one night in a pouring rain, when a car slammed into her while she waited for her ride. Not one to give up, she still waits.

Another apparition that appears in the yard outside the school from time to time is also thought to be an early-day teacher. Unlike Miss Suzette, she is always in a hurry. She appears ever so briefly and vanishes just as quickly.

If you happen to look at the staircase at just the right moment, you might catch a glimpse of a ghostly little girl who happily runs down the stairs, only to vanish before she reaches the bottom. There is also the ghostly janitor who enjoys his cigars. There is no smoking in the building, so if you should catch a whiff of cigar smoke, you'll know the ghostly janitor is nearby. He keeps everything in shape just as he did long ago. He is also known to angrily admonish students when they get too boisterous for his liking. And if you listen very closely on quiet days when the snow is piled high along the edges of the roadway, you can hear them. They are laughing and jumping, running and calling out to one another, just as they did so long ago in this stately old building.

Ghosts of the Washoe Club

*Y*ou can't come to Virginia City on a ghost quest without checking out the Washoe Club. And every ghost hunter knows this. As Cheryl Nicoles, a ghost-hunting buddy of mine, once enthused, "the Washoe Club is the mother ship for ghost hunters." She was right, of course. If I had a dollar for every time I'd investigated ghosts at the Washoe Club . . .

Take a seat at the bar, or a table; there's always a convivial atmosphere here, especially if you're talking about the ghosts who hang out upstairs. Countless celebrations and paranormal events have taken place at the Washoe Club. And these, no doubt, will continue. Just about every paraceleb in the field has investigated the upstairs of the Washoe Club. Many have donated their items to the museum. The Washoe Club is historically interesting on many levels, especially ghost hunting. This is where Zak Bagans and *Ghost Adventures* not only filmed a full-body apparition but also got so scared that they ran screaming from an upstairs room.

In the days long before Zak, Nick, and Aaron became TV's ghost-hunting stars (*Ghost Adventures*), they came to Virginia City for a live ghost hunt. I was fortunate enough to be invited by Zak to help with the event. I asked to bring my friends Mark and Debby Constantino, and luckily Zak said yes. We were so excited to take part. We wanted to try something different, so we devised an experiment in which we would attempt to gather ITC (instrumental transcommunication) during the séance that was to be held in the ballroom. The experiment was to see whether we could capture photos of the dead on a TV screen while we sat in our circle and called for any and all spirits to join us. There was nothing conclusive.

However, provoking did go on. And one participant was slapped by an unseen force. Nick got sick, and one woman was possessed by the spirit of a small child. In other words, wherever you are, whatever you do, don't provoke! You might get some nasty results you weren't expecting, especially upstairs at the Washoe Club.

Lena, the Lady in Blue

A most unusual attraction at the Washoe Club is the spiral staircase that one time served as the entrance to the Washoe Club from the Crystal Bar. The staircase has been listed in Ripley's Believe It or Not! as being similar to the mysterious Loretto stairs in Santa Fe, New Mexico, in that there is no center supporting pole, but it doesn't have as many turns. The staircase is a popular spot for selfies, and while you're at it, keep a close eye out for the beautiful ghostly Lena. It's on this staircase that she is most often seen.

Lena was a young prostitute who some believe died here in the Washoe Club. If you don't find her at the staircase, remember that she also likes to stare out from the bar mirror. Don't be frightened if you should look up from the bar and see her smiling out at you. Is it possible for ghosts to do that?

Look at it this way: If a ghost has overcome death and is able to appear before and communicate with the living, what can't they do? Probably not point out which Megabucks machine is set to pay off.

Did Lena Laugh at Them?

*L*aughter is common to haunted locations. I'm not sure why this is, unless the ghosts are having a good laugh at our efforts to find and communicate with them.

Like so many other groups, RASS (Reno Apparition Seekers Society) members Jeff Frey, Jason Ball, and Bruce Pollard were so intrigued with their first overnight investigation of the Washoe Club that they returned to conduct another overnight investigation.

They felt that Lena was with them through most of their investigation. During an early morning EVP (electronic voice phenomena) session, they got what they considered proof when they captured a woman's soft laughter. When asked what was so funny? The ghost remained silent. What was she laughing at? They are convinced Lena was laughing at them. Was she?

Debby Constantino at the Washoe Club

*T*he Washoe Club was a favorite of the late EVP specialists Mark and Debby Constantino. It was here that I introduced the charismatic Constantinos to Zak Bagans and *Ghost Adventures* for the first time. The rest is TV ghost-hunting history.

The Constantinos considered the Washoe their home away from home. A number of their Con-Cons (paranormal conferences) were held at the Washoe. Their tragic murder-suicide deaths in September 2015 stunned the paranormal world. Since that time, several people have told of seeing Debby's apparition in the ballroom upstairs at the Washoe.

When the ghostly Debby is spotted, she is wearing a glowing royal blue dress much like that of Lena. As she happily spins around, she asks, "Isn't my blue dress pretty?"

Although some people say they have captured his voice as EVP, no sightings of Mark have been reported thus far. A Class A EVP of him clearly saying his name was captured by his sister during a special investigation on the first anniversary of his and Debby's deaths.

On September 21, 2016, a group of us were gathered at the Washoe Club for an interview on Darkness Dave Schrader's radio show—Debbie Bender, owner/operator of Bats in the Belfry Virginia City Ghost Tour, my husband Bill and me, and one of Mark's sisters and his brothers. After the interview, we went upstairs to attempt to communicate with the Constantinos. Mark's sister was using some of the very same recording equipment that Mark and Debby had once used. After a short recording session, she replayed the recording, and there was Mark's voice saying the word "Mark."

As we listened in awe, a woman suddenly screamed from somewhere in the distance.

"That's coming from the bar," someone said. If that were the case, one of the four recorders being used would have picked up the scream. But none did. "Maybe that's Debby," someone else said.

"Debby, is that you? Are you angry that you're not getting any attention? Say something to us, please."

Silence . . . if Debby was present on that night, she didn't see the need to speak to us.

The Millionaires and the Man Who Shot Himself

*Y*ou may be wondering if any of the millionaires who struck it rich in the mines haunt the Washoe Club today. Why not? If ghosts can go anywhere they want (and I believe they can), one or two may have decided to return.

Some of the members of the Millionaires' Club included silver baron John Mackay, president Ulysses S. Grant, and writer Mark Twain. According to Lucius Beebe in his book *Legends of the Comstock Lode*, the Washoe Club was the scene of a stupendous dinner in honor of President Grant.

When the mines stopped producing, the silver rush was over. The silver barons took their money and opted for other cities. By the 1930s, the upper floors of the building were converted to apartments. According to some, it was in one of these converted apartments that a man shot himself. The story goes that he was so overcome with grief over the death of his young son that he couldn't go on. Don't expect his ghost to be friendly. Whenever he appears to ghost hunters, he seems angry and agitated. He has also been known to shove and push anyone who gets too near him.

The Museum

$\mathcal{T}$he museum at the Washoe Club is one of the few paranormal museums in the country. It offers a fascinating collection of photos and ghost-hunting memorabilia and equipment. Stop at the old coffin. No touching. Get a picture; try to get some K-2 readings and EVP. This is one of those places where you can sense ghosts all around you the moment you step inside.

Did you see the shirt Zak Bagans wore in his first documentary? It's here in one of the cases. Incidentally, the documentary runs continuously in the museum. If you've forgotten anything about it, stop and watch. And if you start to feel a chill in the air, remember, the Washoe Club is haunted, and ghosts do wander in and out.

Several St. Patrick's Days ago, Debbie Bender, owner of the Bats in the Belfry Virginia City Ghost Tour, presented an event called the Black Shamrock in the museum. The event included a meal, interesting talks, and a séance. While the meal was wonderful and the talks thought provoking, the séance was lively and informative. We got activity: some names and dates that later proved true.

The Crypt

$\mathcal{T}$he crypt is one of the strangest locations at the Washoe Museum. If you're wondering how it came to be called "the crypt," there's a story about that. According to a long-told tale, bodies were stored in this area of the building when the ground was frozen solid and no one could dig a deep enough grave. The bodies stayed here until the spring thaw came, making it possible to dig graves. There are those who will tell you this is the absolute truth. And then again, there are those who insist this is nothing but an oft-told legend meant to titillate and frighten all who visit the crypt.

People are sometimes touched, feel their hair played with, or hear words whispered in their ears in the crypt. I know of a group of experienced investigators who did an overnight investigation at the Washoe. There were five grown men in the group, and not one of them wanted to do an EVP session alone in the crypt.

There may be a ghost by the name of Hank whose favorite spot is in the crypt. My friend Richard St. Clair, former tour guide at the Washoe Club, happened to be in the crypt with a psychic one day when she told him that there was a ghost called Hank next to him. During the Comstock era, there was a famous stagecoach driver named Hank Monk who lived and died in Carson City. His ghost has long been haunting the Lone Mountain Cemetery in Carson City. And maybe he occasionally wanders up the hill to Virginia City, as he did in life.

Taking a Ghost's Advice

*D*uring an overnight ghost investigation at the Washoe, a young couple left the group and wandered down to the crypt to be alone and do a private EVP session. Hoping for amazing evidence, they spent several minutes calling to any and all ghosts to join them and communicate with them.

Their words were met with only silence. Still, it was all good, and they were enjoying themselves even though they'd captured nothing on their recorders. In desperation, the woman finally said, "We're going to stay right here until someone talks to us!"

At that moment something touched the woman's face as she recorded the words "Better leave now."

And they did, no questions asked.

Bathroom Ghosts

*Y*ou'd think a ghost could find a better place to haunt than a bathroom. But for some reason bathrooms are very popular with ghosts. Go figure. The hauntings in the Washoe Club's bathroom have been going on since before *Ghost Adventures* arrived in Virginia City. And it seems to be the work of a child or a prank-playing ghost. There is a ghost on the premises who sometimes locks women in the bathroom.

If you should overhear people wishing each other good luck before visiting the bathroom, now you'll understand why.

Something Shoved Her Down the Stairs

*W*ord is out—the Washoe Club is haunted. Before it was remodeled, the Washoe could be a very tricky place to investigate. Still, an investigation of the upstairs area was de rigueur for every ghost hunter that came to town. With its weak flooring and gaping holes, this could be a dangerous proposition. When you walked into the ballroom, you really had to keep your eyes open lest you step in one of the holes and fall through the floor. But ghost hunters are fearless. And the investigations continued.

The following is a cautionary tale among ghost hunters. During a conference, a small group was in the ballroom trying to collect EVP. After several sessions, they gave up and carefully headed down the back stairs. A woman in the group got the surprise of her life when an unseen hand suddenly shoved her, causing her to miss her footing and stumble down the stairs. There she was with a sprained ankle and no one to blame except a hateful ghost who haunts the upstairs of the Washoe. We all know how often someone records the words "get out" during an EVP session. If only this woman had taken those words seriously that night.

Communicating . . . or Not, at the Washoe

*F*riends attended a conference at which participants attempted to communicate with resident spirits of the Washoe Club using their K-2 meters and mediumistic abilities. They communicated with a female spirit who claimed to have been a young prostitute. Suddenly she was gone. Is anyone else there? The question was quickly answered by the meter's flashing lights. It seemed that a man was there and anxious to speak from the afterlife. Someone heard the name Jack. Yes, his name was Jack.

Someone else got the impression that he was abusive toward women, not the sort of spirit that endears itself to us. This caused some consternation among the investigators. Half of the group was willing to let Jack slide on his behavior now that he was a ghost. The other half said no way.

Becoming a ghost doesn't automatically elevate one to a kinder status. In other words, an evil man in life would certainly be an evil ghostly man. Or would he? That was the question they pondered. The second floor of the Washoe Club was used as apartments for many years. There have been numerous sightings of a man who attempts to frighten ghost hunters. Among the EVP that have been collected at the Washoe Club over the years is the voice of a man who snarls the ghostly stock in trade: "Get out!"

Was this Jack? Some have claimed to be scratched by demons in the Washoe Club. I don't think so. I believe any scratches to be the work of Jack, or some other ghost just as nasty as he is. Knowing this, wouldn't it be best to ignore Jack altogether? Now think about that. If you want no dealings with this sort of person in life, why would you want to communicate with them after death? That night my friends decided to cut their communication session with Jack short and move on to another area of the Washoe. Not all pizzas are good, and neither are all ghosts.

Drink Up, Old Miner

*T*he story of the grizzled old man who occasionally appears at the Washoe Club bar has been told for more than seventy years. According to the tale, he is known for sneaking sips of patrons' drinks. At least this is what he's been accused of. One remedy (works for me) is to buy an extra drink and let it sit next to yours.

But your kindness won't be repaid; this isn't turnabout. Don't ever expect the old miner to buy the next round. When it's time to pay the barkeep, the old miner vanishes into the night air.

Ghostly Footprints

*O*ne afternoon, a friend and I stopped into a busier than usual Washoe Club, only to be regaled with the tale of the mysterious footprints that had just appeared on the floor near the spiral staircase. This was long before ghost hunting became regular TV-viewing fare. Ghost hunting hadn't yet achieved an air of sophistication thanks in part to all the electronic equipment that is continually coming to the market.

Being a small town, Virginia City's news travels fast. Word had already spread up and down C Street about the strange occurrence that had taken place at the Washoe Club. Some who heard the tale laughed the whole thing off. But those who believed in the spirit realm felt their curiosity rise to a fever pitch.

And they came to the Washoe Club to see the footprints for themselves. Whose were they? The general consensus was that they were those of a child, a ghostly child who is usually spotted upstairs. Yes, they were small. But I couldn't help thinking that this was a prank on the ghost-believing populace. Either that, or they were the footprints of a long-ago woman who somehow materialized in our world for a brief moment in time to step across the wooden floors of the Washoe Club. For posterity, I took a few photos with my Sony Mavica and called it good.

As far as I know, this was the first and last time the mysterious footprints made an appearance at the Washoe Club.

The Monkey and the Ghosts

*T*he *Sacramento Daily Union*, July 1, 1873, reported on a tragic explosion in Virginia City:

TERRIBLE EXPLOSION IN VIRGINIA CITY, NEV. TEN PERSONS KILLED AND MANY WOUNDED. SEVERAL BUILDINGS BLOWN UP AND BURNED. VIRGINIA, NEV., JUNE 30TH. There has been a terrible explosion of giant powder in Root's building. The building was burned. The two upper stories of the bank building were also burned out. Ten persons were killed. The fire is out. [SECOND DISPATCH.] Additional Particulars—Names of the Killed and Wounded. Virginia City, June 8th. Last night, at 10:45 o'clock, a terrible explosion of nitroglycerine and giant powder occurred in this city near the corner of Taylor and C streets, killing ten persons and wounding many others. A large number of bodies are missing, and probably buried beneath the debris. The explosion, it is supposed, was caused by six cans of nitroglycerine exploding without any apparent cause, and the concussion of that exploding 150 pounds of giant powder, all of which was stored in or beneath the room of General Van Bokkelen, who was agent in this city for giant powder. The following buildings were shattered and partly thrown to the ground: Bank of California and buildings to the rear of it, Kennedy & llallon's grocery store, Douglas' building, used in the upper apartment as a lodging-house, Daly's saloon and Armory Hall.

The Washoe Club is housed in the Douglas Building. According to legend, one night General Jacob Van Bokkelen's pet monkey was playing with the general's nitroglycerin, which he kept under the bed. The monkey wasn't smart enough to know the danger, and caused the disaster. Is it such a leap to assume that some of the ghosts who wander here in the Washoe Club are a result of that long-ago blast? Did the monkey cause the catastrophe? Possibly, but thus far there have been no reports of a ghostly monkey running amok. If you'd like to pay your respects to the brave but foolish General Jacob Van Bokkelen, he is buried in an unmarked grave in Virginia City's Silver Terrace Cemetery.

What the Medium Felt

*M*y friend Deborah Hollingsworth is a gifted medium. We've traveled all over the country investigating ghosts. So many haunted places, and yet she'd never been to the Washoe Club. I felt remiss having not shared one of Northern Nevada's best places to explore the paranormal with her. My conscience was assuaged and the problem solved one spring when our friend Richard St. Clair, a tour guide at the Washoe Club, graciously agreed to give her a tour of the upstairs area.

Like others, she felt a lot of activity on the stairs that was so negative it made her uncomfortable. On the second floor, she sensed a lot of people milling around, gambling and drinking.

"Was a mortician here?" she suddenly asked.

Richard nodded.

"I feel like he visited here often, or maybe an office. Did he?"

Well, there is the crypt downstairs, but that's not what she meant. I clarified this with her later. "That mortician had business in one of the upstairs rooms. Either he worked or stayed there. His presence was just too strong."

"Was he a nice man?" I asked.

Deborah smiled. "No, I didn't feel this. But his clients never complained. And he did like his job."

That's some consolation, I suppose.

Then there were the horses. She sensed horses being taken up and down the back stairway. "Something like after races," she said.

Hmm, I wonder if it had been a horse that shoved (or nudged) women down the stairs.

She agreed with Richard and just about everyone else: The real negativity resides on the third floor. "There is definitely not a feeling of comfort and coziness up there," she said. "Someone committed suicide here. No, I feel that there was more than one."

Richard told of a time on the second floor when he looked up and saw legs dangling from the ceiling. I think that could be from the third-floor hanging. A despondent man supposedly hanged himself there.

Her psychic impressions finished, we sat at the bar and enjoyed a glass of wine.

Did the Doll Scare You?

*T*here is a doll upstairs that some people believe is haunted—either that or it is possessed by a playful spirit. A young woman bravely went upstairs at the Washoe Club by herself one rainy afternoon. Her intention was to record EVP.

She came running down to the bar area a short time later claiming that the doll was haunted; its eyes had moved while she was photographing it. She had no EVP for her trouble, and a blurred picture was no proof that the doll's eyes had really moved. Others claim the doll scares them just because of the way it looks.

Certainly the doll is creepy and old and could probably tell a lot—if she wanted to. But is she haunted? One way to find out is to do an EVP session with her. Just don't say I didn't warn you.

Ghost Hunting Back in the Day

Ghost hunting may be popular TV fare, but it is nothing new, as this February 16, 1906, story from the *San Francisco Call* attests:

COMSTOCK MINERS GO ON GHOST HUNT: Alleged Visitors from Other World Cause Considerable Annoyance. Special Dispatch to the *Call*.

RENO, Nev. Feb. 16. 1906—Residents of the Comstock are very much wrought up over the antics and strange performances of alleged spooks. "The ghosts" seem to inhabit the deserted shafts in the old mining district and each evening terrorize the people in that vicinity by their weird cries and by running, clad in white robes, from one shaft to the other.

So much trouble has been caused by the ghosts that a posse of citizens has been organized for the purpose of either capturing them or making them quit the locality. The more sober-minded residents of Virginia City are of the opinion that jokers are trying to see what the superstition of some of the residents will lead them to do. A few others are firm in belief that the "ghosts" are the departed spirits of former comrades who have crossed the Great Divide.

The Ghost of Arthur Perkins Hefferner

*O*n March 24, 1871, when he believed that Bill Smith had insulted him too harshly, Arthur Perkins Hefferner pulled his revolver and shot Smith through the eye at the saloon in the International Hotel. Fatally wounded, Smith stumbled a few feet and dropped to the floor dead. Hefferner was immediately taken to jail. But the vigilante group known as the 601 wanted retribution and was not satisfied to wait for a trial.

A senseless murder had taken place in their city, and the killer must pay. Early in the predawn hours while most of the town slept, the vigilantes broke into the jail and escorted Hefferner to his doom. By all reports, Arthur Perkins Hefferner didn't utter a word or cry for mercy as the group stealthily led him up A Street to Sutton and on up to the Ophir Mine.

There, the vigilantes quickly lynched him. His lifeless body was discovered hours later. A note was pinned to his coat that read, "Arthur Perkins—Committee No. 601."

Perkins might have been forgotten, but he was not gone. Four months later, the ghost of Arthur Perkins made an appearance, according to the *Stockton Independent*, July 27, 1871.

> Perkins Ghost Appears to a Boot Black—we copy this ghostly affair from the *Virginia City Enterprise* of July 21st.
>
> City jailer Higbee informs us that the ghost of Arthur Perkins, hanged some months since by the Vigilante Committee, appeared the other night to a boot black confined in one of the back cells of the station house for kicking up some kind of row. The boy begged for the love of heaven to be let out of the cell. At first Higbee thought he was trying to play him a trick and

would not let him out; but when he again called, and begged and prayed to be let out that the ghost was again visible, he opened the door and the lad came out as white as a sheet. In order to try him, Higbee told him that the only place he had for him was in a cell with a crazy man who was violent. The boy said he would go and offered to go anywhere to get away from the ghost. As the boy's offense was trifling and he was frightened out of his wits, Higbee let him go.

Wright Stuff Antiques

*T*his one is special to me. It's where I'm usually found on Tuesdays selling books and other treasures. There are six of us vendors in this cluttered and cozy store that offers everything and anything. There's even a ghost named Annabelle. She goes by other names as well, but I like "Annabelle" for the young lady who's said to be dressed in a frilly yellow dress. Although some have seen her as an older woman rocking a baby, these particular stories concern the youthful Annabelle.

One cold and rainy afternoon in the waning days of November, I was at the shop with my husband, Bill, and Mr. Bill, who's been there nearly forever. The boardwalk was wet, and no one was out and about. An eerie stillness hung over the city. The three of us were at the front of the shop, each lost in our own thoughts. Suddenly a loud bang came from the back of the store where Cindy keeps much of her finery. The two Bills and I went in different directions in search of the source. Nothing was out of place, not a door, a dress, or a knickknack. Could have been this, could have been that, we told each other. A little while later the noon whistle blew. Noontime, and all was well on the Comstock (Virginia City and nearby Gold Hill).

We were deep into sandwiches when in walked a weary and somewhat wet woman. She looked around and finally made the decision to purchase a delicate tiny tea set from Nancy's booth. As I rang her up, she said, "You've got glass all over the floor in that back spot."

News to us. When she was gone, I went back to look. And sure enough, there was glass everywhere. A picture had fallen from the wall, shattering its glass. But how? And more importantly, why hadn't we seen it when we were back there? I looked at the back of the picture. The hanger was secure. I looked at the hooks on the wall; they were secure as well. The only way this could have happened was . . .

"Annabelle," I said softly. "I know you did this. And I don't think it's very funny. Please don't do something like this again."

We swept and vacuumed the glass up and rehung the now glassless photo. That's been more than a year, and the photo hasn't come down since.

While she hasn't done this again, Annabelle did appear to a trio of young women one sunny afternoon. They'd asked about ghosts, and I'd told them about Annabelle. They smirked and headed back to where she is most often spotted.

"Annabelle! Annabelle!" they screamed from Cindy's area. "Annabelle's gonna get me!" They raced up to the front counter. "Aren't you afraid?" one of them asked. Clearly she was terrified.

"No," I answered. "Did you see her?"

"Yes!" she cried.

"They say she's a very sweet ghost," I assured her.

She looked at me as if I had lost my mind. "I'm getting outta here," she said, stomping out the door, followed closely by her two friends.

Mr. Bill, aka the man in the top hat, is a nonbeliever who scoffs at the notion of ghosts. One of these days, Annabelle's going to disabuse him of such thinking.

Curious whether the Wright Stuff was truly haunted, my friends from the San Francisco Ghost Society, Tommy Netzband and Anthony Anderson, recently brought the latest and greatest ghost equipment to the store. After dinner, we all headed down the boardwalk and into the store. Tommy and Tony set up their gear in the area where Annabelle is said to reside, and the investigation began.

The SLS (structured light sensor) camera showed not one but three ghosts. The name "Pat" was received in an EVP session as well. Three ghosts—that was exciting. A few months later, Zak Bagans and the Ghost Adventurers came by to say hi. I proudly led Zak back to the area that is favored by the ghosts, telling him about the evidence collected by Tommy and Tony. He stopped a moment and looked around. "It could be a portal," he said.

Yes, I thought. A portal, and like the women in the room of T. S. Eliot's classic "The Love Song of J. Alfred Prufrock," the ghosts come and go.

The Store on the Other Side of the Breezeway

*W*right Stuff Antiques is located on one side of the Virginia City Mall. On the other side of the breezeway is Just Because Gifts. While claiming not to believe in ghosts, a previous owner of the shop told me about a mysterious couple she encountered at a glass case near the front door one afternoon.

In Virginia City, people dress in varied styles and garb. It is not uncommon to see someone in clothing from many different periods. So it was that this couple wore styles of the 1930s and chatted amicably with the shop owner. She turned to adjust a small heater that stood nearby, still talking to the young man and woman. When she turned back to them, they were gone.

"There is no way they could have gotten out the front door and past me without me seeing them. This heater was between us and the front door. They would have had to walk through it," she said, and then hastily added, "I can't explain it, but I still don't believe in ghosts."

Another story concerns some of my books that the owner had displayed at the front door. As one customer stood near the doorway ready to leave, he pointed to the books and said to the owner, "Ghosts! How silly. There's no such thing."

At that moment the display of books fell to the floor, one at a time. The owner laughed when she told the story. "I don't know how it happened. But he scampered out of here in a big hurry."

All I will add to this story is the fact that antique and secondhand stores are full of the belongings of those who've passed on. Perhaps a ghost has decided to stay with her colorful collection of pickle castors. Another may not want to give up his elegant timepiece. It's reasonable that they would make appearances from time to time.

The Cigar Bar and Julia Bulette

*T*his favorite locals' hangout was once a mortuary. And that's a fact. It's haunted. Some say that's a fact as well. Now for the legend—because if there's anything Virginia City is lacking, it's certainly not legends.

The legend here concerns Julia Bulette, a Virginia City prostitute who gained posthumous fame and notoriety because of the senseless way in which she died. She is probably Virginia City's most famous ghost. Everybody has a theory about Julia Bulette. Dead more than 150 years, and Julia continues to be the source of many a bitter argument. A hotly debated argument regards Julia's appearance. What did she look like? The accepted likeness of Julia is a photograph that shows a somewhat austere, pale woman in conservative clothing, with a fireman's belt encircling her waist. Those who believe this is Julia won't be dissuaded by the photo of a pretty, biracial young woman that hangs behind the bar in the Bucket of Blood Saloon.

I disagree with both viewpoints. In my opinion, neither the white woman in the fireman's belt nor the biracial Julia is indeed the legit Julia. I'll take this a step further and say that we will probably never know for sure just what Julia Bulette looked like.

Each of those who've witnessed the ghostly Julia describes her differently—naturally. Julia is also one of those ghosts who make appearances in different locations. And this brings us to another mystery concerning Julia Bulette. No one is sure where she rests. But there are some who claim to have seen a ghostly woman in a long gray dress near what is purported to be Julia's grave. This, they say, is Julia trying to show people where she actually rests. Then again, this ghost could be someone altogether different.

The legend continues with a local undertaker admiring Julia from afar. As the story goes, while preparing her body for burial, the undertaker had an idea on how to keep Julia ever near him. He secretly buried her in the basement of his establishment and then filled her coffin with rocks and sent it off on the funeral cortege. That's the story.

Today that basement belongs to the Cigar Bar on C Street. Over the years people have reported all manner of weirdness happening down in the basement. Is it Julia Bulette? No one knows for sure.

People have been reporting seeing the ghostly Julia for years here at the location of the Cigar Bar. Those who've seen her have described her as being attired in a brown woolen dress and a deep bottle-green cloak. A former owner told me of being startled by the ghost one morning as she opened the shop. Believing the ghost to be a living person, the shop owner wondered how she'd gotten in. And then it dawned on her. This was no living person. She watched silently as the ghostly Julia came right up to her as if to speak, then slowly vanished.

Like so many other ghosts, Julia is said to roam. Besides the basement of the Cigar Bar, she has been seen in the old red-light district area on D Street where she was murdered in her bed in 1867, and at the Flowery Hill location where she is supposedly buried.

Julia fans will be happy to know that she was recently honored by a statue, carved of a long-dead tree that stands in front of the Canvas Café in Virginia City. Perhaps one day, or night, she may choose to haunt this spot as well.

Union Brewery

*T*he story is that there's some bad juju here in the basement. A nefarious ghost is especially active there and in the owner's upstairs apartment. The spirit is said to possess women, lift a bed a foot off the floor, and otherwise be a terrible roommate. But don't take my word for it. In 2020, Zak Bagans and *Ghost Adventures* did a lockdown in the basement and encountered all sorts of nastiness. You'll have to watch that episode to see what I'm talking about.

I will tell you that I had the back of my blouse grabbed while I was visiting Dawn Grant, one of the owners, upstairs during a recent Labor Day parade. Broad daylight, no one was standing near me, and something or someone from the great beyond tugged at my blouse. I jumped. Wouldn't you?

This is a fun place. There's always something going on—karaoke, anyone? Stop in for a drink and a look-see, and someone's bound to tell you all about the ghosts.

Silver Terrace

*T*he Silver Terrace Cemeteries on the north edge of town was created in 1860 and encompasses thirteen cemeteries. Put away your ghost-hunting equipment; the gates are locked promptly at dark, and ghost hunters are neither encouraged nor welcome to conduct investigations in the cemetery. That doesn't mean there aren't ghosts lurking here.

One occurrence that I am familiar with took place nearly twenty years ago and involves my good friend Deborah (Debbie) Hollingsworth, a gifted medium. Debbie and I met at the Silver Terrace early one spring morning. No sooner had she gotten out of her vehicle than she started walking to the edge of the cemetery. Here she announced that there were two children, a little boy and a little girl who was a few years older. I'd already heard the story of the two kids who'd died nearby. Debbie's description fit what I'd previously been told by another medium. Surprising to me, since this was the first time Debbie, a Southern girl, had ever visited Virginia City.

Local lore holds that there is a glowing headstone here in the cemetery that is visible from many locations throughout the town on full moon nights. There are a few explanations as to why the headstone glows. One is of a ghostly nature, of course. According to this tale, the headstone is that of a woman who rises up from her grave, glowing, on certain nights. There is also the explanation that the headstone is actually ghostly glowing children who come out to play on certain nights. Those who disagree say there is nothing ghostly going on here. The headstone, they say, glows because of the material it is made of.

I personally like the ghostly glowing woman story better myself. Regardless, the Silver Terrace is an interesting historical location to visit—during daylight hours. Recently a caretaker's cottage was moved from another location and converted into a cultural center at the cemetery gates. Chock-full of information on life and death during the Comstock era, it should be your first stop before beginning your walk through the old cemetery. Wear comfortable shoes and bring water; the Silver Terrace is more than twenty-five acres.

Bonanza Saloon Ghost Hunt

*O*n a warm summer night on the Comstock, Bill and I were set to investigate the Bonanza Saloon. The wind, like it does on the hill, had suddenly kicked up and was wreaking havoc with everything not tied down.

With us were property manager Sabrina Morgan and a group who'd never gone ghost hunting before that night. The investigation was a favor for a friend, and we were eager to collect evidence that might impress the newbies. We stepped inside, happily forgetting the wind. First stop was the Suicide Table, which during renovations at the Delta Saloon is here. There are so many dark legends concerning this old faro table. Things like shootings and suicides and knifings. None of the newbies knew the stories.

Those who claimed sensitivity to such things stepped up to run a hand across the glass-enclosed table. Their expressions told us that they were not feeling anything pleasant. One of them shivered when told of Jack Palance and his long-ago TV show visit to the Suicide Table.

Next up, we did a quick EVP session and asked the standard question: Is there anyone here who would like to speak with us?

Sabrina had her equipment. We waited and listened as it randomly tossed out a string of words. None made much sense. So upstairs we went. Yes, heat rises, and yes, it was very hot up there, except for a corner room that was suspiciously cold. There were no fans or air conditioners up there. The room was cold for a reason—and that reason is usually a ghost. Sabrina's equipment gave us another string of words.

She informed us that a well-known medium who had investigated the room said that a woman was stabbed there in the stomach. We hastily made a plan to research that story and the building's history. It was hot and cramped in the hallway. We moved down to the basement where Sabrina pointed out the spot where Zak Bagans stood during his and *Ghost Adventures'* investigation there. Out came the phones, and a few photos were taken. Then it was down to the subbasement (nothing more than a crawl space, where even the shortest among us had to duck). The men chose not to go inside. The women stooped and stepped in.

Surprisingly it was hot down there. How was that possible with heat rising? Hot or not, this is where the ghostly action is, I thought.

Sabrina said, "Last year someone got EVP that said, 'I was buried down here in 1859.'"

The historian in me wouldn't let that slide. "This building wasn't even here in 1859; none of them were. That was the year when silver was first discovered at Gold Canyon, and this was nothing."

Even in the dark with only phones for light, I could see their faces. And they were telling me I'd just ruined a good story. "That's not saying that someone wasn't buried here—I mean, they could have been. Yes, that must be it! How could anyone dig a grave when they couldn't even stand up straight down here?"

That seemed like a logical point to me. I took a photo of a streak of light that I couldn't explain. Sabrina's equipment said more words, and we decided to conclude the investigation.

I'm not sure if the newbies were impressed or not, but still I believe the Bonanza Saloon is haunted. However, on this night, the ghosts were ambivalent to us, giving us a big meh, a yawn, and all that. I've always thought that ghosts don't sit around waiting to entertain ghost hunters. On this night, they proved that we are as unnecessary to their world as they are to ours. The ghosts here are not eager to jump through hoops at our command. And that's part of the fun. You never know if you will be bombarded with activity or met by jaded ghosts, bored with you and your equipment.

Obviously these ghosts were not in the mood to entertain us. They've got their existence, and we've got ours.

Daddy's Ghost

*N*owadays ghosts generally appear in the local newspaper during the Halloween season. Things were different in the nineteenth and early twentieth centuries. It was not unusual to find a ghost story throughout the year.

The November 12, 1872, issue of the *Territorial Enterprise* carried the following story, titled "The Talking Ghost":

> A girl of fourteen, named Agnes McDonough, living on North C Street, has had the spirit of her father, who died six years ago, appear to her on several occasions recently, so that she could see him and hear him speak. The spirit was not seen by any others than herself, yet he could be heard talking to her. The young lady and her parents being Catholics, the resident priests in Virginia and Gold Hill were informed of the circumstances, and have investigated the matter pretty thoroughly. They have conversed freely with the spirit, and express both conviction and astonishment. Other gentlemen of reliability also attest to the fact as stated.

Reporting on the story two weeks later, the *Inyo Independent*, November 30, 1872, stated,

> The spirit came back for the prayers of the faithful. He had been in purgatory six years, but was to go to heaven in six days. At the time set, the daughter saw the spirit depart. A pair of shining wings being unfolded as he took his leave.
>
> Within the past few days, Dr. S. A. McMeans, a well-known physician of Virginia City, has also been

visited by a ghost or two, who, or which, have promised to reveal to him some immense silver deposits; conditions not named, if this promise is realized, spiritual stock will go up like a rocket.

Agnes McDonough, whose parents were both dead, lived at her aunt's home on C Street. On Sunday, October 27, 1871, the ghost of Agnes's father came calling indeed—but only when Agnes was alone. Dead six years, he appeared just as he had in life and was anxious to speak with his Agnes. Not sure what to make of what was going on with her, the family consulted Reverend Father Manogue, the vicar general of Nevada.

The *Gold Hill Daily News*, November 25, 1872, reported on Father Manogue's visit to Agnes McDonough with the following:

Catholic Spiritualism: The Virginia City Ghost Again

The *Catholic Guardian* of last week contains the following report from Reverend Father Manogue the Vicar General of Nevada to the Bishop of the Diocese Bishop O'Connell Marysville, which we considered of sufficient interest to our readers to copy in full:

I thought I would inform you about a strange occurrence which took place here on Tuesday, October 27th. There is a girl named Agnes McDonough living with her aunt, to whom her father (dead about six years) appeared. The apparition continued from Sunday, October 27th, to Friday November 1st appearing to the child whenever she was alone in the house or in any room of the house.

The article went on to say that the ghost appeared and spoke, and looked as he did in life. Reverend Father Manogue questioned Agnes and the family and gave her a series of questions of a religious nature to ask the ghost. The ghost answered, claiming he'd been in purgatory and explaining the importance of religious adherence. When asked about Spiritualism, which happened to be the current rage, the ghost proclaimed it nonsense.

The Tragic Jones Boys

*T*here are two ghostly young boys who are said to roam the Gold Hill Cemetery during heavy winter snowstorms: fourteen-year-old Henry Jones and his nine-year-old brother, John. The youngsters froze to death on the Ophir Grade during a raging Christmas Eve blizzard in 1871. More than 150 years later, the circumstances that led to their deaths are still debated.

One story holds that their father, Bob Jones, was a cruel disciplinarian who sent the boys out in the snowstorm to find one of the family's lost horses, telling them not to return until they had the horse. Jones, it was said, thought nothing of beating his children if they disobeyed him. The children, fearful of being so harshly punished, went out into the blizzard.

Local newspaper editor and journalist Alf Doten subscribed to this belief and wrote a scathing story about Bob Jones after the boys' deaths.

Others said Doten was wrong in his assessment of Bob Jones and his sons' deaths. They believed the boys were on their way to the Comstock from the family ranch in Reno when they lost their bearings, got disoriented in the ensuing blizzard, and froze to death.

The Jones boys were buried in the Gold Hill Cemetery, and a headstone was placed upon the grave. A hundred and three years later, in 1974, a hiker in the area photographed the headstone. Sometime later it disappeared from the cemetery. Using the hiker's 1974 photograph, a replica of the headstone was created and placed upon the Jones boys' grave. Ten years after the replica headstone was created, the original headstone was discovered in Petaluma, California (244 miles from Virginia City). After cleaning and restorative measures, the original headstone was once again erected on the Jones boys' grave, adding an amazing postscript to the tragic story of the two little boys who perished in a long-ago snowstorm.

Séances and Spiritualism were very popular in early-day Virginia City. It's not surprising that a local spiritualist/medium went into a trance in June 1872 and reportedly received messages from the two little boys. Alf Doten was sitting in the séance circle and claimed that contact was definitely made with the Jones boys that night and that the boys were happy in the afterlife far from the hand of their cruel father.

Some believe that Henry and John Jones are the two glowing figures sometimes seen playing in the Gold Hill Cemetery.

Ghosts at Priscilla Pennyworth's Old Time Photos

*P*riscilla Pennyworth's Old Time Photos is one of those photo studios that encourage customers to do a little role-playing. Whether you want to be a cowboy, a saloon girl, an old-fashioned lady at teatime, a Wild West lawman, or any number of characters, they've got you covered. With their old-fashioned costumes and settings, the shop is perfect for those who want to have an *authentic* photo taken of themselves as a Virginia City souvenir.

If you can't come up with a great photo idea yourself, look around—the walls are covered with photos of previous customers. Then, too, there are the employees, friendly and ready with fun ideas. If you're curious, one of them may even tell you about the shop's ghosts.

This is Virginia City. You'd be hard-pressed to find any building that doesn't have at least one ghost lurking about. There was a ghost here that liked to grab a former owner by the ankles as she walked up or down the basement stairs. Believing her ghost to be a child, she didn't think much about it—until the day the prank-playing ghost tried to shove her down the stairs. Upon hearing this, an employee quit that very day, vowing never to step foot in the basement again.

And the hauntings continue. Recently a medium visited Priscilla Pennyworth's Old Time Photos and told of seeing two elderly women in the back of the shop. She attempted to speak with them, but the ghostly ladies ignored her entirely. Ghosts are like the rest of us; they don't necessarily want to talk with everyone.

My friend Angie has had better luck with the shop's ghosts. She's an empath and new to ghost hunting. With a bubbly personality that matches her bright red hair, the enthusiastic Angie charms customers and ghosts alike. She's been able to carry on conversations with a ghost who calls himself Nick, and to get a doll, which some claim is haunted, to calm down. This isn't to say that Nick isn't frisky and hasn't grabbed Angie's behind a few times—he has.

But after Angie firmly told him that this was not appropriate behavior, the ghostly Nick seems to have calmed down.

Who Haunts the Horton Mine?

*T*he stories of the haunted Horton Mine are all over the internet. And here I will offer a word of caution—never go into an abandoned mine; stay out at all costs. Nevada's landscape is dotted by numerous abandoned mines, but they are dangerous. Many things can go wrong, and people have lost their lives while exploring them.

Yes, there are stories of mines being haunted—I'll take their word for it.

The Horton Mine outside of Yerington is an abandoned mine that is said to be very haunted. Founded by William Horton about the time Nevada gained statehood, the mine was said to have produced some gold and silver ore for the next seventy years. When the ore gave out, the mine was abandoned and forgotten. This doesn't mean that a miner, or two, might not have wandered in and gone away with a nice little share of ore.

They may have. Or they may have met their deaths for one reason or another there in the depths. And some of them may have stayed on to haunt the Horton Mine. Eerie sounds are said to emanate from the mine, and there is that glowing figure that has been seen around the mine entrance. Who is haunting the mine, and why, are two questions that will no doubt remain unanswered. Ghosts can be frightening, but abandoned mines are always deadly.

Reno

Reno

Reno is the Biggest Little City in the World. The smaller of Neva-da's two most famous cities, Reno is located in the northwest part of the state, approximately five hundred miles north of Las Vegas. Founded in 1868, Reno's history is tied to its early industries: railroads and gambling.

Luis Ortiz

Luis Ortiz is an angry ghost. Luis's story is a tragedy that should never have happened. And this may be the reason that the ghostly Luis is said to angrily wander the bridge to this day. Time has passed, and there have been two bridges to replace the old iron one that Luis was lynched at on a September night in 1891.

Luis was a rowdy Winnemucca ranch hand in town enjoying a night of drinking when he got into an argument with two other men, stabbing them both. Constable Nash put Ortiz on a westbound train, and Luis promised to never return to Reno. If only he had kept that promise.

A few months later, Luis Ortiz was back in Reno and drinking heavily. When he pulled his gun and started shooting, a bystander went for Constable Nash. While subduing the drunken Luis, Constable Nash was shot in the stomach. Luis was taken to jail as doctors awaited Nash's imminent death. But the secret vigilante group known as the 601 had no intentions of waiting.

The masked group devised their evil plan. When they were sure that no one was out and about, they went to the jail and forcibly removed Luis. Dragging him to the iron bridge that spanned the Truckee River in downtown Reno, they urged him to say his prayers, for he was soon to die for killing Constable Nash.

After throwing a noose around his neck, the men hoisted him up onto the bridge. His body was taken down the next day. Miraculously, Constable Nash made a full recovery. Is it any wonder that Luis Ortiz is an angry ghost? Is it any wonder that his ghost has haunted every bridge that's taken the place of the old iron bridge where he was cruelly lynched?

Ghost in the TV

*W*hen I started writing *The Big Book of Nevada Ghost Stories*, my son Fred and his wife, Peg, asked that I share the story of their haunted TV. I gave a noncommittal answer and continued writing.

"You should tell the story, Mom, because," Fred said, "it's true."

We'd discussed the TV many times, and after thinking it over, I've included the tale of the haunted TV.

The star of this story is a vintage color TV circa 1970s or 1980s, with a large twenty-five-inch screen and a nice boxy wooden cabinet. The TV had belonged to Peg's late mother, and no one in the family could bear to toss it out. But then no one wanted the monstrosity in their home either. So it made its way to Fred and Peg's house.

The first time the old TV set turned itself on, with the volume turned up high, they thought it was a fluke. And that was the end of it. The TV was put in the spare bedroom and forgotten about. And then one night they were watching a TV show about ghosts, and Peg asked Fred, "Do you remember the time my mom's TV went on by itself? Do you think it was haunted?"

Before Fred could answer, there came a noise from the spare bedroom. The TV had turned itself on, and the volume was all the way up. Did this mean a ghost was attached to the TV? Was it Peg's mom, or someone else? They weren't sure—and it was too late to try and make sense of it. Peg turned the TV off, and they went to bed to ponder the haunted TV.

Fred and Peg have since moved to another state. The TV went with them.

Fred recently told me, "That TV turned itself on every time we mentioned it."

"Where is it now?" I asked.

"In the basement, and it's unplugged."

"Does it still turn itself on?" I asked.

"I don't know. But I can tell you that we're always very careful not to mention it when we're in the house."

Ghosts in the Courthouse

*N*evada has a propensity to demolish old buildings and rebuild new ones. This is especially true in Las Vegas and Reno. Consequently, unlike other states, Nevada may not have many haunted theaters. But as we'll soon see, the state has a lot of haunted courthouses. The Washoe County Courthouse in downtown Reno is said to have several ghosts wandering its floors.

Justice has been dispensed at this location since 1873. The first courthouse to sit here was a two-story brick building; it was within this old building that the hauntings began with a woman named Olivia Miller. Mrs. Miller was the widow of a man who'd been battered to death by an axe. George DeLong, the handsome handyman, explained to the sheriff that he'd killed Mr. Miller in self-defense. The sheriff was nobody's fool—seeing the looks that passed between the widow and the handyman, he promptly arrested them.

DeLong went to jail. But the jail was not equipped to handle female inmates, so what would they do with the widow? It was decided that she would be locked in the district attorney's office on the second floor of the new courthouse. Being a strong woman, Mrs. Miller broke the lock on the door and escaped within the week. When they found her, she was taken back to the district attorney's office, and the lock on the door was reinforced. But there was a window. And no one thought that anyone, much less Mrs. Olivia Miller, would attempt an escape through it. Unfortunately, she did. On September 2, 1876, Olivia Miller opened the window and looked out. It wasn't that far down. She misjudged her ability and was killed in the fall.

The ghostly Mrs. Olivia Miller is described as a large woman who seems out of sorts. Her apparition has been seen in and around the new courthouse that was dedicated in the summer of 1911. Some say she is here because parts of the original old courthouse were incorporated in the new courthouse. And that could well be. It could also be that the ghostly Mrs. Olivia Miller is still trying to figure out what went wrong with her escape plan.

Two years later, Joseph Rover was hanged in the courthouse courtyard. February 19, 1878, was such a cold morning that those involved didn't want to spare the condemned man another moment. As they hurriedly went about the business of hanging him, Joseph Rover insisted, as he had for days, that he was innocent of the crime he was being executed for. No time. Snowflakes were coming down at a furious pace. Rover had had his appeals; there was nothing more to say or do.

Today the courthouse annex takes up that area. And yes, Rover is said to be the ghostly man who is encountered in this area of the courthouse. People who've worked there claim to have felt unexplained icy cold breezes. A darkly unhappy man who vanished the moment he was spotted is believed to be either Joseph Rover or one of the men who were shot to death in the courthouse in 1960.

If Rover truly was innocent of the crime he was hanged for, he could be angry at the circumstances of his death. His anger may account for the ghostly shrieks and moans that are said to echo through the building late at night when the nine-to-five crowd has gone home. Twenty years after Rover's execution, a man who gave testimony against him was rumored to have made a deathbed confession claiming that he was the actual murderer.

By far the eeriest place in the courthouse is the old jail upstairs. The jail hasn't been used since the 1970s, and having been up there, I can tell you that I believe the stories of the long-dead inmates that slam the iron doors open and closed and wander through the jail. One person told me that although he didn't believe in ghosts, he realized there was something weird going on up there. I shivered while examining the cells on a hot summer day. When my hair was touched, I jumped, assuming it was Bill. But he was standing several yards from me. Okay, then. I took notice.

Just being confined in such a place would have been punishment enough, and possibly enough to frighten even the hardest of criminals onto a law-abiding path.

Haunted Car

In 1965, there was a short-lived sitcom called *My Mother the Car*, starring Jerry Van Dyke. The premise was that Van Dyke's character owned a car that was haunted by his deceased mother. And she talked to him through the car radio. I know. It does seem silly when looking back at earlier TV fare, but this doesn't mean that cars can't be haunted. As an example, I offer up this tale that was shared with me by a blackjack dealer many years ago.

> If only my husband had been able to stay off drugs, he might still be alive. Instead, he died in jail a couple of days before his thirty-second birthday. After he died, I started driving his Caddy for the first time. The car was old and needed some repairs, so I took it in and had it fixed. After that, it was like a brand-new car. I always felt so close to him whenever I drove it. He loved that car.
>
> But I never realized just how much he loved it until the night I was driving back to Reno from my sister's house in Sacramento. Just as I passed the Gold Run exit, I turned on the radio to help keep me company. An old favorite of mine came on, and I started singing along with it.
>
> Then someone said, "Change the station."
>
> "I will not!" I said to myself, because I was alone in the car.
>
> "You know I hate country music," he said.
>
> I glanced over at the passenger seat, and there was my husband.
>
> "Now I know I'm tired," I said aloud.

He laughed. "You didn't think I'd give up my Caddy that easy, did you?"

"This is some sort of dream or hallucination!" I screamed.

He blew me a kiss and was gone.

I broke all the speed limits getting home that night. And you better believe I sold that car almost as soon as I got back to Reno.

I've seen the car around a couple of times. And he may still be haunting it for all I know.

Ghost on the Narrow Gauge

*T*he railroad that opened up travel across the United States in the nineteenth century is a source of more than a few of Nevada's ghost stories. The narrow-gauge Nevada-California-Oregon (NCO) Railway was built in 1882. From the outset, there were problems with the railway's management and cash flow. In 1880, another problem struck the railway—the ghost of a murdered man who was said to appear at a point on the railway two miles from Reno, on the 27th of every month, and walk along the track.

With a knife still protruding from his chest, the nameless ghost may have been commemorating the date of his death as he silently made his way along the tracks. Some superstitious passengers avoided traveling on the 27th, lest they encounter the ghostly man.

Ghosts on Campus

*H*ave you ever heard of a college or university that wasn't haunted? Neither have I. That said, it should come as no surprise when I tell you that the University of Nevada–Reno has more than its share of ghosts. Founded in Elko (about three hundred miles east of Reno) in 1874, the university was approved for relocation to Reno in 1885 by the Nevada legislature. Since that time, it has been known as the University of Nevada–Reno (UNR).

The UNR campus is a mix of old and new architecture. Completed in 2008, the Mathewson-IGT Knowledge Center, one of the most technologically advanced libraries in the United States, is a short distance from Lincoln Hall, which was reportedly built near an old graveyard. When it opened on January 1, 1896, Lincoln Hall featured electric lighting and running hot water and housed ninety men. One of the young men residing in Lincoln Hall was a twenty-year-old student by the name of James Champagne who died under mysterious circumstances in the winter of 1906.

Popular with his fellow students and professors, Champagne is one of UNR's most famous ghosts. Was his death a tragic accident, a suicide, or a murder? No one was ever quite certain. What we do know is that soon after his death, the ghost of James Champagne was heard sobbing in his former dorm room in Lincoln Hall. The ghostly Champagne has also been seen staring out from an upstairs window. Those who've seen him say he appears to be sorrowful and perplexed. He is blamed for cold drafts and rattling windows and doors that open and close as if by some unknown force. This well could be the work of another ghost altogether.

It seems that Champagne isn't the only ghostly resident at Lincoln Hall. A figural gray mist was seen throughout the dormitory long before James Champagne died. In the early 1960s, a student, despondent over a broken romance, drank cyanide and died in

Lincoln Hall. Years later during a séance, contact was made with the student who occasionally wanders the grounds outside Lincoln Hall. There is also the ghostly little boy who has no explanation as to why he haunts Lincoln Hall, only that he does. It is believed that the child's grave was disturbed at one point during construction on the UNR campus.

Apparently James Champagne isn't content to spend all his time at Lincoln Hall. He seems to be one of those ghosts who aren't content to linger in one location. He was buried in the Genoa Cemetery and occasionally appears to walk among the tombstones there as well.

The Frandsen Humanities Building is located at one of the most picturesque spots on campus, near Manzanita Lake, where turtles, ducks, and swans happily coexist. Constructed between 1917 and 1918, the building is haunted according to employees who've witnessed paranormal activity like cold spots and doors opening and closing by themselves.

Built in 1885, Morrill Hall is the oldest building on the UNR campus. A fun fact about this building is that its architect, noted Reno architect M. J. Curtis, assisted in the design of the Goldfield Hotel as well. The ghost who lingers in Morrill Hall is a young woman who wanders through the old building weeping uncontrollably. No one is sure who she is. And those who've seen her say she seems surprised that she's been spotted. No, she will not communicate or speak into your recorder.

My favorite ghost at UNR is that of Katherine Duer Mackay, daughter-in-law of Virginia City mining magnate John Mackay. The first wife of Clarence Mackay, early-day feminist Katherine was a woman well ahead of her time. In 1909, as president of the New York Equal Suffrage Association, Katherine Mackay asked Jeanne Weir, University of Nevada history professor and founder of the Nevada Historical Society, to create a Nevada suffrage organization. That was the beginning of Nevada's women's suffrage movement.

So how, you may be wondering, did New Yorker Katherine come to haunt the University of Nevada–Reno? It begins with a large endowment the Mackay family bestowed upon the university in honor of family patriarch John Mackay. There is the Mackay

Stadium and the Mackay School of Mines and the statue of Mackay himself outside the school of mining. And there is that large portrait of Katherine herself that was done by John White Alexander in 1905.

Katherine poses holding a crystal ball, and in the forefront of the painting, a spirit rattle, used by early-day Spiritualists, is depicted. The portrait's Beaux Arts tabernacle-style frame also has an interesting history. The frame was specially designed by Stanford White the year before he was shot to death by Harry Thaw for his romance with Thaw's wife, Evelyn Nesbit.

The painting of Katherine was discovered in the basement during the 1988–1992 renovation of the Mackay School of Mines building. There is nothing shocking about that—except that the painting was floating freely in midair.

Legend holds that Katherine herself is attached to the portrait. Former employees claim the painting is imbued with a powerful energy that gives off a strong sense of eeriness. Everyone is very careful when adjusting or moving the painting, lest they irritate the ghostly Katherine.

Donner Ghosts

*T*he Donner Party arrived at Truckee Meadows in what is present-day Reno in the late summer of 1843 and made camp at a spot near the base of Rattlesnake Mountain. After the exhausting journey across the forty-mile desert, they wanted nothing but to rest, so they stayed longer than they should have.

Lulled by pleasant weather and plentiful water, the leaders refused to heed the warnings of those who knew the vagaries of the Sierra and had cautioned them: *It's best to cross the mountains now, for harsh snows could come early at any time without warning.* The decision to wait until fall before crossing the Sierra would cost several of them their lives. Many of those who survived did so by resorting to cannibalism.

Today the area where they camped is known as Donner Springs, a thriving southeast Reno neighborhood of houses, condos, and apartments. Donner Park, at the Millhouse Townhomes, is a small neighborhood park near the spot where the ill-fated Donner Party camped. Nearby, a small monument honors those who lost their lives in crossing the Sierra. Some who've lived here will tell you that members of the ghostly Donner Party are still around—especially the children.

For many years, ghostly children have been seen playing at the foot of Rattlesnake Mountain in the early morning hours. Now imagine the shock of the woman who woke in the middle of the night to see translucent children at the foot of her bed.

When asked how they were dressed, she replied, "I was so shocked at what I was seeing, I didn't pay attention to what they were wearing."

Experts on such things believe that the little ghosts were members of the Donner Party who have returned to the last area on earth where they knew peace and hope.

Ghost at the Grocery Store

*Y*ou never know when you're going to be told a ghost story. That said, I'm nearly always assured to hear about a local ghost when I do one of my Famous Ghosts classes for Truckee Meadows Community College. So it was that a woman who'd recently attended the class shared this story with me. It has all the earmarks of an urban legend, but so do many ghost stories.

The cities of Reno and Sparks have grown and expanded so that the cities are next to one another. Sparks is the smaller of the two, and it is here in a large supermarket that our haunting takes place. A shopper who died near the soda aisle has apparently chosen to stay on at the store. As they are shown the ropes, new employees are casually warned about the ghost they call Clara.

If you're afraid of ghosts, the soda aisle may not be your favorite place to hang out—even if they call for a cleanup on that particular aisle. Clara likes things nice and quiet. When the canned grocery store music is accidently turned up a notch, she reacts by pushing items off the shelf. High prices are bad enough, but when loud music is added to the mix, Clara reacts. When someone irritates her, she is not above throwing something at them.

Some employees have even blamed Clara as their reason for turning in their resignations. After all, a cantankerous ghost goes beyond quiet quitting.

Haunted Houses

All houses in which men have lived and suffered and died are haunted houses.

—Mary Roberts Rinehart

*A*s a ghost researcher, I am often told about haunted houses. The stories range from outlandish to intriguing; none are more interesting than those that have made their way into local newspapers. The Pedercini house was such a haunted house.

The little house stood on the northwest corner of West and Second Streets and was surrounded by tall trees. According to Mr. and Mrs. Pedercini, the house also had a ghost.

The April 5, 1906, issue of the *Nevada State Journal* carried a story about the haunted house titled "Another Visit from the Spook." In the story the newspaper stated, "G. Pedercini and wife declare that their home is surely haunted by a ghost. Fact of the disturbance is not to be doubted, but nobody knows the cause of the disturbance."

And that was probably the Pedercinis' biggest question. Why was their ghost so angry and destructive?

The article continued:

> The skeptical will say it is a "fake ghost," but Mr. and Mrs. G. Pedercini still maintain the presence in their home of an immaterial spirit who knocks things down and has terrorized Mrs. Pedercini.
>
> The ghost's antics happened at exactly 7:30 PM— while the family sat in the dining room with their three-year-old daughter, the ghost began throwing dishes in the kitchen.
>
> Pedercini, who declares he is afraid of no ghost, rushed to the scene of the racket and found that the

84

performance of other evenings had been repeated. Kitchen utensils had been loosened from their pegs on the wall and were lying in a heap on the floor. Everything was quiet, and the visitor had evidently taken its departure.

The Pedercinis told the newspaper that they intended to move from the haunted house, and eventually that is exactly what they did.

Our next haunted house also appeared in a local newspaper. Is it haunted? At least two previous owners thought so. The house is located on Court Street in downtown Reno. The old Tudor-style home was built in 1912, a bygone era. Not many people require homes this large in downtown Reno anymore. For this reason, and because of its short distance to the Washoe County Courthouse and other businesses, the mansion is now used as office rentals. Perhaps the ghosts from long ago still reside within the old building.

A previous tenant of the building told of hearing the sounds of a ghostly party and of champagne glasses clinking together in broad daylight. When he walked into the room to see what was going on, the room suddenly fell silent. Another tenant claimed his dog did not like going near the stairs. Whenever he got close to the stairs, the dog would stop and stare, then slowly slink away.

They say animals know when a ghost is near. And apparently this dog did.

There is also an old house on Court Street that is said to be haunted by a young man who, despondent over a broken romance, hanged himself in the home sometime during the 1950s. Although he is seldom seen, the ghostly man cries and moans and noisily paces back and forth in the bedroom that once belonged to him.

Several blocks south on California Street is a stately old mansion where the same joyous scene is often played out on the winding staircase. A ghostly young woman in a shimmering red dress happily glides down the stairs, her eyes set somewhere in the distance. Who she was and where she was going are questions that haven't been answered. Perhaps they never will be.

Then there was the large house located in southwest Reno. Development and progress have encroached in that area of town so that the house is no longer standing. The house and grounds belonged to a wealthy couple in the early 1950s. They loved their home and couldn't have been happier. But as things sometimes happen, they began to squabble over the smallest of things. They tried to hang on for the children's sake, but clearly they'd fallen out of love with each other. And neither of them wanted to stay married. So the wife filed for a divorce, and because they had young children, she was permitted to stay in the house that belonged to both of them jointly. He didn't protest. He was a wealthy man; he bought another house and eventually married another woman.

The years went by; the children grew up and moved out. Rather than downsizing, the ex-wife stayed in the home she'd raised her children in, the home she loved. She kept the large house spotlessly clean and worked in her flower garden every day. She died in her garden one spring morning while pulling weeds—a heart attack, they said.

As co-owner of the property, the ex-husband was left to sort things out and, with the help of their children and grandchildren, dispose of the ex-wife's belongings. The first time he stepped through the doorway, he was alone. Suddenly he was overtaken by the many youthful memories that filled the old house—hers and his. He could almost smell the aroma of the pumpkin pie she'd baked here on their first Thanksgiving under this roof. And Christmas, all the snow, the tall tree she'd wanted placed near the big bay window. He smiled at how frazzled they'd been as they tried to untangle Christmas tree lights while kids and a big black dog called Homer ran around the tree.

Even though it was spring, he could almost hear a fire crackling in the large fireplace—almost feel the fire's warmth.

"Those were the best of times," he whispered to himself.

"They were," a familiar voice answered.

Startled, he looked toward the spot where the Christmas tree had once stood. The ex-wife was standing there, not as the stooped old woman the years had made of her, but as the pretty and vibrant woman he'd married all those years ago.

He rubbed his eyes. His emotions had run away with him, and his imagination was playing tricks. There was no one in the room but himself. She was dead and buried; there was no way she could be here with him, looking like she once had.

Feeling foolish, he spoke the words he felt compelled to speak: "I'm sorry for every stupid mean thing we ever said or did to each other."

"I am too," came the response.

He stepped out of the room. And there she was, standing near the stairs.

"I haven't had a drink in days. I'm not hallucinating, so what is going on?" he cried.

She smiled. And for the first time he realized that she was glowing and translucent.

"A ghost!" he cried. "You're a ghost!"

"It's all right," she chuckled. "I told you that I'd never leave this house, and I won't," she said, turning from him and slowly dissolving.

The house was empty, cleared of everything she'd ever collected, created, worked with, and loved. His children asked him why he didn't move back into the house. After all, they reasoned, he'd loved the house as much as Mom had.

He couldn't tell them the truth, that their mother's ghost was haunting the place. They would think that he'd taken to drinking heavily. At the very least, they would doubt that he had a firm grip on reality. So he shared his secret with only a few close friends. He simply couldn't move back into that house and live with his ex-wife's ghost. Eventually the house and surrounding acreage were sold to developers. The house was razed, the land was cleared, and a slew of new office buildings were erected. The question is, does a ghostly woman still tend to her long-ago home and garden that once occupied this spot?

Yes, a condo can count as a haunted house. There's a condo in southeast Reno where a heinous murder occurred decades earlier. Some who've lived in the condo since that time have told of hearing sobbing and eerie noises in the living room once in a while. A neighbor's TV, the wind, cats fighting, these could be the source of that noise. But I don't think so. And I bet you don't either.

Marilyn and the Ghosts at Papa's Pizzeria

*P*icture this—a quirky and oh-so-haunted pizzeria where Marilyn Monroe once slept, according to local legend. But wait, the legend gets more intense. Marilyn supposedly cavorted with JFK (John F. Kennedy) here as well. It was summer 1960; Marilyn, Clark Gable, Montgomery Clift, and the crew were in Northern Nevada filming *The Misfits*. Many of the film's scenes were shot at nearby Pyramid Lake.

Why would everyone want to drive back to Reno after a grueling day of shooting? They probably didn't. The story goes—according to Bryan Eidem, owner of Papa's—that while Gable and the others stayed at Crosby Lodge, Marilyn spent her nights here. Local lore has John Kennedy spending some time here with Marilyn.

If you're seeing Marilyn in the kitchen tossing pizza dough, quit it. There were some nice little cabins and cottages out back, and that's where the blonde bombshell stayed. And she well might have. JFK is another matter entirely. At that time, he was knee-deep in a presidential election, so it's difficult to imagine him out here in the middle of the Nevada desert making love to Marilyn. I'm not saying it didn't happen. But if it did, you've got to wonder just how JFK managed to slip away from his security detail, the news media, and the fawning public—not to mention his adoring wife, Jackie.

Recently, Bill and I visited Bryan at Papa's Pizzeria to get the scoop and some tasty pizza. First thing through the door, and it's obvious that Bryan is a collector of the whimsical and the unusual, as well as sports memorabilia. This isn't a bad place for a ghost to hang out, we decide as we tour the property. And yes, this is one of those places where anyone sensitive to such matters can feel a ghostly presence. A few cats, leery of strangers, run from us as if we are demons sent to make all nine lives of resident felines miserable and unhappy. "We're here for the ghosts," we assure the kitties, who remain unconvinced.

Throughout the property, there is the eerie feeling of being watched. It's a feeling that put me on edge. And no, I'm not talking about the cats. We were drawn to the room called Marilyn's Room. There are a lot of old furs and other feminine paraphernalia that a celebrity of Marilyn's status would no doubt have owned back in the day. We spent a few moments looking around and decided to do a quick recording session while Bryan made our pizza.

Bill's EMF meter, aka K-2, gave a good showing when Bill asked if Marilyn was there with us. After asking if it was true that she'd stayed there, we watched as the K-2 lit up.

"Would you like to tell us about it?" I asked.

Apparently that was a no. The recorders were silent.

We said we'd been told that there was a woman ghost there who liked to whisper the names of men who visit the room. Bill introduced himself and waited for the whisper. The pizza was done before the whisper came—in fact, it never came. But the pizza was heavenly, and we were hungry. So we ate our pizza and made plans to return for another pizza and another investigation.

Lake Tahoe Area

Lake Tahoe

Accompanied by Mr. Preuss, I ascended today the highest peak to the right from which we had a beautiful view of a mountain lake at our feet, about fifteen miles in length and surrounded by mountains that we could not discover an outlet.
—Captain John C. Fremont, February 14, 1844

Lake Tahoe straddles the Nevada-California border, and thus both states are proud of the crystal-clear lake that happens to be the second-deepest lake in the United States.

Mark Twain walked from Carson City to Lake Tahoe, an approximately twenty-eight mile jaunt. Of his view of Lake Tahoe, he wrote,

At last the lake burst upon us—a noble sheet of blue water lifted six thousand feet above the level of the sea and walled in by a rim of snow-clad mountain peaks that towered aloft full three thousand feet higher still. . . . I thought it must surely be the fairest picture the whole world affords.

Long before Fremont and Twain sang its praises, Lake Tahoe was home to the Washoe people, who lived on its shores and fished its waters. They held many legends of their beloved lake, which they called Lake of the Sky. Our next story is a retelling of a Washoe legend.

The Wife's Ghost

A young wife died shortly after giving birth to her first child, leaving her husband heartbroken. Consoled by friends and family, he tried but just couldn't get past his grief. One night he left the baby with family and went deep into the woods to plead with his wife's spirit to either return to him or take him with her.

When she appeared, the ghost demanded that he bring her child to her. Happily, he ran back to the village and grabbed the child. Everything would be all right now. She would come back to him, and life would be good once more. But when he found her, the ghostly wife and mother only wanted to hold her child once more.

As she walked among the towering pines, singing softly to her baby, he trailed behind her. Finally she stopped and handed the baby back to him. As he reached for the baby, he tried to touch her.

"No!" she exclaimed. "If you should touch me, you will die as well."

"But we must be together," he protested.

"Go back. You belong among the living. I am no longer a part of your world."

"Then I will go with you," he cried.

"You cannot!" she said, turning from him.

He tried to follow but discovered that she was disappearing with each step until there was nothing left of her.

Back in the village, he told the elders what had happened. They looked sadly upon him and the baby.

"The spirit held this child. It will surely die," they agreed.

"No!" he howled. "Not my child!"

But the elders were right. The baby died within the week.

George Whittell's Home

A man who does not think for himself does not think at all.

—Oscar Wilde

*G*eorge Whittell made his wealth the old-fashioned way—he inherited it. And with all that money at a time when most people were struggling with the Great Depression, George was living well. He had wisely liquidated his $50 million shortly before the market collapse. But there was still the California income tax. In order to escape the dreaded tax, George, who preferred to be called "Captain," came to Lake Tahoe and bought more than forty thousand acres of land, covering twenty-seven miles of Lake Tahoe's eastern shoreline. Here he built the rustic home that would eventually become known as Thunderbird Lodge.

Although he died in 1969, the ghostly George is rumored to still be in residence at the home some have referred to as Nevada's answer to the Winchester Mystery House. Indeed, George Whittell was as enigmatic as Sarah Winchester, with a love of his surroundings and enough money to have a home built to his particular specifications. Unlike Mrs. Winchester, George was not much concerned with the supernatural.

I was fortunate to have visited and investigated Thunderbird Lodge a number of times before it was decided that ghost enthusiasts were no longer permitted to investigate the ghosts who linger here at this rustic home on the shores of Lake Tahoe. During many investigations, EVP was recorded in various areas of the lodge. One of the most intriguing was in the boathouse where the sound of Native American chanting was heard by some investigators. This land had once belonged to the Native Americans, and legend has it that ghosts remain here at Thunderbird Lodge as a way to demonstrate their unhappiness with what has been done to their land.

Among the spectral residents is George Whittell himself, and a workman who died when he fell from a ladder while working on an indoor pool. After the death, Whittell wanted nothing more to do with the pool and ordered the room sealed up. Another ghost is that of a cook by the name of May. Rumor has it that she and Whittell were lovers. When she died in a car crash, he never got over his broken heart. True or not, May stays on. She may be the ghost who's been known to shove people in the boathouse if they should speak disparagingly of George Whittell.

Legend has it that George kept a pet lion he called Bill on the grounds. Legend also has it that the ghostly lion Bill has been known to nuzzle those he likes.

Thunderbird Lodge is truly a location with a multimillion-dollar view; is it any wonder that ghosts would stay on?

Biltmore Mary

*A*t this writing, the Tahoe Biltmore has been purchased and is slated for demolition. And this has me wondering where this will leave the ghostly Biltmore Mary.

The Tahoe Biltmore was one of the first hotels to be built at Crystal Bay after the state of Nevada made gambling legal on March 19, 1931. Twenty-seven years later, gaming magnate Lincoln Fitzgerald, owner of the Nevada Club in downtown Reno, purchased the hotel and changed its name to the Nevada Lodge.

Under Fitzgerald's direction, the Nevada Lodge became one of the most popular places at Lake Tahoe. The building was remodeled and enlarged, with a new addition that included a showroom. With the remodeling came the need for new and exciting entertainment. Rumor has it that Lincoln Fitzgerald had an eye for a pretty girl. It didn't take him long to decide on Vive les Girls, a French revue that featured nude and scantily clad beautiful young women, to perform in the new Topaz Room. Naturally the show was a big hit.

Lincoln Fitzgerald died in 1981, and his Nevada Lodge was sold and renamed the Tahoe Biltmore. Gone forever was the Topaz Room and Vive les Girls. But one dancer was said to remain on the premises. She was known as Biltmore Mary. As part of their orientation, every new employee was told about Mary, who was said to have been a dancer with the Vive les Girls revue. Her lover was believed to have been a married man who held a management position at the Nevada Lodge.

The story is that when her lover broke up with her, the heartbroken Mary killed herself. There are several versions of how Mary met her end. One has her going to her room and taking a bottle of sleeping pills. Another has the distraught young woman racing her car down the icy Mount Rose Highway, only to lose her life when the car plunged off the highway, throwing Mary from the vehicle to her death.

The old showroom was converted to a wedding chapel. Mary chose to stay here and make herself a nuisance. She would turn lights off and on and cause a cold breeze to waft through the room just as the bride and groom kissed each other for the first time as husband and wife.

While no one ever actually saw Mary, they knew when she was nearby. A man who claimed not to believe in such things changed his mind one night when he was working alone in the stage area. A woman's soft laughter followed him as he made his way down the hall and onto the empty stage.

"Okay, Mary. I know you're here and you're real," he said aloud.

The laughter stopped. Perhaps acknowledgment is really all the ghostly Mary ever wanted.

Frank's Piano

*T*he Cal Neva at Crystal Bay was owned by singer/actor Frank Sinatra for a time in the early 1960s. Directly across the street from the Nevada Lodge, the Cal Neva sat on the shore of Lake Tahoe. It was here that stars appeared in the acoustically perfect showroom designed by Sinatra himself. And it was here that Sinatra entertained his Rat Pack cronies, Sammy Davis Jr., Dean Martin, Joey Bishop, and Peter Lawford. Beautiful blonde actress Marilyn Monroe was a good friend of Frank's who visited the Cal Neva so often that she was assigned her own cabin.

Rumor was that Marilyn continued to haunt her cabin many decades after her death. There was a couple who, up until the time of its closing, visited the Cal Neva regularly for one reason—to stay in Marilyn's cabin and communicate with her spirit. What they discussed with the dead screen star, they never said.

Several years ago, I was doing an investigation at the cabin with a small group of friends. One of them captured EVP that said, "Breathless."

Did the voice sound like that of Marilyn Monroe? Yes, but that isn't really proof that Marilyn had spoken across the veil and said the word "breathless." What was amazing to me was the fact that someone managed to get a photo that looks eerily like Marilyn Monroe in total darkness.

The Cal Neva Lodge offered an idyllic setting among the tall pines and huge boulders near the water's edge. If only Sinatra had played by the rules. The Nevada Gaming Commission rules stipulate that no person listed in the Black Book is permitted entrance to a gaming establishment. Mafia member Sam Giancana was listed in the Black Book. And yet his pal Sinatra allowed him to come into the Cal Neva so that he could be closer to his lady love, Phyllis McGuire, of the popular trio the McGuire Sisters.

It was 1963. Marilyn Monroe was dead and buried in Brentwood, California. Before the year was out, President Kennedy would be assassinated in Dallas, and Sinatra would be forced to forfeit his gaming license and his beloved Cal Neva.

Fast-forward to early 2000, and the Cal Neva was still operating. Sinatra, who'd been dead a few years, was still the hero and the resident ghost. Women tell of having him kiss them on the cheek, call out to them, and on occasion tug at their skirts. The owners of the Cal Neva brought a piano that once belonged to Old Blue Eyes to the showroom from Hawaii. And that's when the hauntings took on an even stronger Sinatra flair. A life-size photo of Sinatra disappeared from the showroom first. And then there was the piano music that was heard in the wee hours of the morning. The tunes were always those that Sinatra sang—"Strangers in the Night" and "My Way" were two of the most often recognized.

"If you are near his piano and speak to him, he will respond," employees assured each other. And all agreed that Frank indeed responded when his name was spoken. Usually it was nothing more than a soft caress on the shoulder. But there was that one time a new employee parked in Frank's assigned parking place. The employee drove up and turned off the engine.

"It's all baloney, Frank Sinatra," he said. "You're dead, and you don't need a parking space."

He stepped out of the car and was slapped sharply across the face by a person or persons not of this world. Do I have to tell you that he jumped back in the car and moved it to another location, promising never to take Mr. Sinatra's parking place again?

Washoe Valley, Genoa, Carson City, and the Carson Valley

Washoe Valley

*T*he Washoe Valley was named for the Native American tribe, the Washoe. Located midway between Reno and Carson City, it was here in the Washoe Valley that the nouveau riche silver-mining millionaires Sandy and Eilley Bowers built their Bowers Mansion in 1863. The Bowers' story is one of the most enduring in the Northern Nevada region.

Tip the Ghost Dog

Old Galena was a mining town south of Reno that began with a silver discovery in 1860. The town was ideally situated between Lake Tahoe, Carson City, and Virginia City. And as the need for lumber in mining operations increased, Galena boasted eleven lumber mills. After two disastrous fires, the town was abandoned in 1867. It is here in Old Galena where the ghost of Tip the dog appeared one night.

George R. Peckham was an elderly man in 1922. From childhood to middle age, he had lived in Old Galena. When asked by the *Reno Gazette-Journal* about Reno's ghosts, Peckham remembered an encounter with Tip.

> About twenty or twenty-five years ago we had a little black dog which we called Tip.
>
> At that time a band of sheep was being pastured in a field near the house, and the coyotes being quite plentiful, the sheepherder put out poison. Tip found some of it and was poisoned and died. About one week afterwards, while I was driving home from Reno one moonlight night, my old gray horse stopped suddenly when a black dog that looked just like Tip jumped up at his head, the same way as Tip had done before nearly every time when I hitched up the old gray horse to the buggy to start for Reno. The horse saw the dog and dodged his head as he had often done before. I watched the dog until he seemed to vanish a short distance from where he had jumped at the horse's head, and I thought at the time that it must have been Tip's ghost, which was seen by both the horse and myself.

I have seen and felt some very remarkable phe-nomena of a little different nature from the above, and am convinced that there are many forces in nature that science knows little or nothing about, and many scientists and students of nature freely admit that such is the case.

The House Where Eilley Bowers Lived

*S*andy Bowers was one of the first silver miners on the Comstock to strike it rich. Not long afterward, he and his landlady, twice-divorced Eilley Orrum Cowan, were married. Eilley had always believed in what she saw in her peep stone (crystal ball), and she'd seen the bright future that lay before her and Sandy. The hardscrabble life was a thing of the past for both of them. Spending was suddenly no problem.

And as Sandy boasted, "We have money to throw at the birds."

But even as she slipped into her life of luxury, Eilley realized that one day she would live in poverty once again. *Rags to riches, riches to rags*, the peep stone had shown her.

As wealthy as the Bowers were, the one thing they were lacking was a fine home. Urged on by well-meaning friends, the Bowers began to consider having a mansion built for themselves. And Eilley knew just the location for her new home. It was the spot in Washoe Valley where once Eilley had scrubbed clothes for miners. Eilley had owned the land since 1856 when she and her second husband, Alex Cowan, purchased it.

Here is where the Bowers Mansion would be built at the unheard of cost of $300,000. In order to furnish their home, Eilley and Sandy traveled to Europe on a buying trip. No expense was spared as they selected fine woolen carpets, art treasures, and costly furniture. A longtime legend holds that the Bowers Mansion was fitted with silver doorknobs.

Shortly after they returned to their home, tragedy struck when Sandy died unexpectedly of pneumonia in Virginia City at the age of thirty-five. Eilley was devastated. After a lavish funeral, she looked at their finances. She had a daughter to raise and expenses to take care of. Unprepared for the financial mess Sandy had left her in, Eilley quickly realized that Sandy had made some disastrous financial moves and left her penniless—most likely she would lose her mansion.

While Eilley devised one plan after another to hold on to the mansion, death came into her life once more when her beloved daughter Persia was suddenly struck down with a fatal childhood illness. The child was buried in the family plot on the hill overlooking the mansion. And on the day of the funeral, Eilley solemnly climbed the hill, telling herself that one day she would rest there too. Filled with sorrow, she thought of the loss of Sandy and of Persia. She could not go on.

Somehow Eilley realized there was no other way. She found the strength to admit defeat and moved from the mansion. Let the creditors, like vultures, pick her financial bones. Because of the generosity of friends and her ability as a fortune-teller, she would not go hungry or be homeless. In Virginia City once again, she was sought out and paid well for her ability at scrying (gazing into the crystal ball) to see the future.

As she grew old and frail, Eilley became deaf. She could no longer speak with clients and was often made fun of and ridiculed. With most of her friends long dead, there was nothing else for Eilley to do but seek help from the US government. After all, she reasoned, she and Sandy had given the government $14,000 to help the union cause. Her claim was ignored, and she was sent to the poorhouse in Reno. From there she was sent to the King's Daughters Home in Oakland, California, where she died on October 27, 1903. Because of the generosity of a local businessman and his wife, Eilley Bowers's ashes were brought back to Nevada and buried beside Sandy on the little hill that looks out across Washoe Valley.

It wasn't long afterward that the glowing lady ghost was seen scurrying across the grounds by motorists near Bowers Mansion at night. Nothing to worry about. It's only Eilley Bowers checking up on her property, they assured themselves. The ghostly Eilley has been spotted in and around the mansion many times since her death. She is sometimes accompanied by Persia and a child who is said to have drowned in the water fountain many years ago.

Persia is most often seen in the mansion, usually by children. There is the story of a little girl on a preschool field trip who encountered the ghostly Persia.

"I once lived here," Persia informed her.

"Was it fun?" the little girl asked.

"Oh, yes," Persia responded.

When the little girl's mother came into the room and joined her, Persia vanished.

"I was talking to a little girl who used to live here," the child told her mother happily.

"That's nice," the mother answered absently.

They walked into another room, and the little girl gasped. "That's her! That's the little girl I was talking to," she said pointing to the portrait of Persia.

Genoa

*F*ounded in 1851, Genoa is Nevada's oldest settlement. It was also the site of Nevada's Constitutional Convention in 1859 and is located in the Carson Valley at the foot of the Sierra Nevada. The quaint little town is famous for its annual Candy Dance event that brings thousands of visitors every September. "Candy Dance" is a cute name and one that might have been apropos when the event was first held as a fundraiser in 1919. Today, what's really going on here are the arts and crafts. Artists and craftspeople come from all over to show and sell their stuff. And it's a fun day for everyone.

Visitors can explore the Mormon Fort museum, the courthouse museum, the cemetery, antique shops, restaurants, and the oldest bar in Nevada. If time hasn't stood still here, it's certainly slowed down.

The cows that graze in their pastures, the deer that wander town streets unafraid, the mountains and the trees—it's all very bucolic. But there's a dark, ghostly story here.

Adam Uber's Hanging Tree

It's said that revenge is a dish that's best served cold. This is especially true when it comes to a vengeful ghost.

The tale of Adam Uber is Genoa's oldest ghost story. Uber was lynched on the edge of town by a drunken mob on a wintry November night in 1897. Uber was in jail charged with murder and awaiting his trial when an angry mob cut telephone wires and took the law into its own hands.

The night before, Adam Uber and Hans Anderson, a well-liked Genoa man, were drinking in a Millersville saloon. Both men had had too much to drink when they got into an argument over money that Anderson claimed Uber owed him. Uber denied the debt, and Anderson angrily slapped him. Tired of being bullied by Hans Anderson, Uber pulled his pistol and shot the other man in the heart.

Many of those in the mob who broke into the jail that night had witnessed the killing. They knew Uber was a murderer. And that was enough. It was well past midnight when the mob headed toward the jail. Emboldened by a long night of drinking, the masked men rushed the jail, catching the sleeping Sheriff Brockliss and Constable Gray off guard. The lawmen were plainly unarmed and outnumbered. As Brockliss and Gray stood helplessly by, Adam Uber was pulled from his jail cell and dragged naked up Boyd Lane, screaming for mercy.

At gunpoint, Sheriff Brockliss and Constable Gray were made to accompany the mob to a stand of tall cottonwood trees. One of the men quickly slipped a noose around Uber's neck. And as the moon dropped beneath the mountains, the other end of the rope was tossed over a sturdy tree branch. Without further ado, Uber was hanged.

Struggling and gasping for air, Adam Uber cursed his killers and their families into several generations for the cruel death they were inflicting upon him that night. The bloodthirsty mob's response was to pull out their guns and fire several shots at the dying man.

The next morning, Adam Uber's lifeless body was discovered still swinging on the branch of a cottonwood tree. No one claimed to know anything about his death. The coroner's jury found that Uber met his death at the hands of unknown parties. And while most Nevadans were horrified at the lynching and demanded that something be done about it, Genoa returned to normal and went about its business. That is, until the angry ghost began appearing at the cottonwood tree where Adam Uber was lynched. One by one, the men who'd been involved in Adam Uber's death either lost their lives or saw their family members perish in bizarre accidents. A leader of the lynch mob died in a runaway horse accident at the very spot where Adam Uber was lynched. Several took their own lives, and two saw their children die horrific deaths.

They say the ghostly Adam Uber is either in the old jail cell where he spent his last night on earth, or there at the cottonwood trees, and that he appears on moonlit nights to relive that terrible night when a crazed mob took his life without benefit of judge or jury.

Adam Uber, Is That You?

*U*pon hearing this story many years ago, I set out with a ghost-hunting pal in search of the ghostly Adam Uber. It was just turning dark when we arrived in Genoa; most of the town's visitors were gone. We parked at the Mormon Station, and with flashlights in hand we started walking down Genoa Lane, taking the same route the mob had taken.

Our imaginations were in high gear as we imagined the horror and fear Uber had surely felt. When we reached the grove of cottonwoods with the sign announcing that this was the hanging tree, we stopped and, using our flashlights, read,

> On this tree early morning November 25 1897 occurred the blackest episode in the history of Nevada. Adam Uber of Calaveras Co. Cal was forcefully taken from jail . . .

Terrible, we agreed. "Adam Uber, are you here?" my friend asked the tree.

"Would you like to speak to us?" I asked, gazing at the full moon that had risen.

Suddenly there was a rustling in the grass—and a deep growl.

"Maybe I'd better tell him that we aren't related to those who did this to him," my friend said and proceeded to repeat her sentence loudly.

The rustling continued; so did the growling.

"I think it's him," my friend said. "But why is a ghost hiding in the grass?"

"Could it be a bear?" I asked. "Aren't they supposed to be hibernating?"

"Adam Uber, is that you?" I asked one more time.

"It might be a bear!" my friend said. "Let's get out of here."

And down Genoa Lane we ran, promising each other that next time we would look for the ghostly Adam Uber in his old jail cell.

Nevada's Oldest Thirst Parlor

*E*stablished in 1853, the Genoa Bar and Saloon is the oldest in Nevada. Judging by outward appearances, this little saloon might not seem like a place that's been visited by so many famous people, but it is. The list of those who've stopped here to slake their thirst includes western actors John Wayne, Richard Boone, and Clint Eastwood; singers John Denver, Johnny Cash, and Willie Nelson; comedian Red Skelton; and actress Raquel Welch. And there's a story, albeit not ghostly, about Ms. Welch's visit here.

Several years ago, Raquel Welch was making a movie at Lake Tahoe when she came down to Genoa for a bit of relaxation. The beautiful actress stopped in at the Genoa Bar and noticed all the bras hanging on the walls. She asked the bartender why they were on display, and he explained. And then he had an idea. Would Ms. Welch be so kind as to leave her bra here for all to see?

She thought about it and agreed, on one condition. All the other bras must be taken down. Hers would be the only bra to hang at the Genoa Bar. He saw no problem with the movie star's bra being the lone such item. "Okay," he said.

And the rest is a story they tell at the bar.

People love the rich old western ambiance here at the Genoa Saloon; it's rare to visit and not find the place crowded with fun lovers. Some of them are of the ghostly variety. The tales are varied and get more so as your beer glass is refilled. There is the ghost who likes to give employees a bad time by moving glasses and equipment around. He is a prankster and friendly to all. The man who is rumored to have hanged himself long ago in a nearby building is not. It's been said that he likes to stare in the large mirror in hopes of frightening anyone who might want to admire their reflection too long. Hmm, I wonder if he's considered photo-bombing selfies.

Genoa Cemetery

Is this picturesque old cemetery haunted? Spend an afternoon wandering through the Genoa Cemetery, and you stand a good chance of encountering a group of deer that like to roam throughout Genoa. Once the sun goes down, your odds of meeting up with a ghost increase. Many of Nevada's earliest pioneers rest here in the Genoa Cemetery, which is just about a mile from Genoa on the Jacks Valley Road. Among those interred here are legendary Norwegian American John Albert "Snowshoe" Thompson who delivered the mail between Genoa and Placerville, California, from 1856 to 1876, and David E. Walley who developed Walley's Hot Springs Spa in 1862. Incidentally, Walley's Hot Springs is still going strong. But it's the ghosts we're here for, and one of my favorites is the ghost dog.

You may not see him, but you'll know the ghostly canine is nearby when you hear his bloodcurdling howls. Was he a lost pet or a lonely stray dog that died nearby? No one knows for sure, only that he is often heard within the cemetery. But how do we know this isn't a real fur-and-blood dog out for an evening stroll among the headstones? I asked that same question of the person who told me this story.

She laughed. "Nothing earthly howls like that!"

I'll take her word for it.

Before we leave, let's remember another resident here. He is James Champagne, whose tragic story ended at the University of Nevada–Reno campus. Some believe he is the shadowy young man who is said to walk weeping through the cemetery. He is like many other ghosts who like to wander from one place to the next, so he divides his time between Genoa and Reno.

Manoukian Professional Building

*T*he Manoukian Professional Building in Gardnerville is listed on the National Register of Historic Places. Built in 1914 by Dr. E. H. Hawkins to serve as Carson Valley's first hospital, the building has been used for many different purposes. The hospital closed in 1924, but because of its location, it was converted to a boarding house for those who taught at the high school across the street. For the next twenty-four years, the brick building would be used as the teachers' home.

Local lore has it that during that time, a young teacher was killed by a speeding car while crossing the street early one evening. Unaware of her sudden death, the teacher has stayed on, haunting the building.

In 1948 the boarding house closed, and the building would sit vacant for the next thirty years until new owners took it over and decided to restore it. In 1985, Nevada Supreme Court justice Noel Manoukian and his wife Louise bought the building. And that is where our story begins.

A group of ghost-investigating friends and I visited Louise Manoukian at the Manoukian Building after prior arrangement in the summer of 2001. It was early evening and hot—still hours before darkness descended on the building. As we pulled into the parking lot, one of my friends said, "Look! Look up there! There's a woman in an old-fashioned nurse's uniform. She's waving to us."

I looked, but I saw nothing. Inside she pointed to a photo on the wall. "That's the woman who was welcoming us here," she said.

"Nurse May Kinney," Louise answered. "Yes, she is believed to return and check up on the old hospital from time to time."

Someone wondered aloud if she might be the ghostly woman who tickles children who visit the building. While doing EVP, we asked this ghost who she was but received only laughter. There was sadness about the building. This had been a hospital. People had come here at joyous times in their lives; they'd given birth and left the hospital with babies and fond memories. Others had come at their lowest moments. Some recuperated. Some were not so fortunate. They'd died here. Perhaps that was the reason for the feelings of heartache and sadness.

Was the ghostly woman Nurse May Kinney or the teacher who met an untimely death as she crossed the street? It could have been either one. On this night, we all agreed—it was Nurse Kinney, and she'll be here for a long while.

Nevada Governor's Mansion

*T*rick or treat! If it's Halloween, head down to the Governor's Mansion in Carson City. There you'll find that the mansion is decorated in all its spooky glory for the special holiday. On the front stairs, the governor and the first lady will be handing out candy to Nevada's children. It's a long-held tradition. You see, Nevada was admitted to the Union on Halloween, October 31, 1864.

Nevada was a state rich with silver, but it was slow in creating a home for its governor. After attaining statehood in 1864, it would be another forty-five years before the Governor's Mansion was completed in Carson City. In July 1909, Governor Denver Dickerson and his wife Una moved into the stately mansion at 606 Mountain Street. The Dickersons' daughter June was born in the mansion that same year. As of this date, June Dickerson is the only child to have been born in the Governor's Mansion.

In 1911, Denver Dickerson's term was finished, and the family moved out. Or did they? Although many Nevada first families have resided in the mansion, the ghostly Una Dickerson and her daughter June are believed to be the two resident ghosts. Both have been seen throughout the mansion countless times over the years. Una appears in a long flowing white gown holding the hand of June, who, although she died at age fifty-three, appears as a young girl of around seven years old. They don't say a word but gaze solemnly at their surroundings.

Another ghost story associated with the Governor's Mansion is that of the haunted grandfather clock. Several years ago while giving me a tour of the mansion, a caretaker pointed out the old clock and informed me that it was haunted. Apparently a ghost had come with the old clock when it was moved from the state capitol to the mansion.

"Even the air around the clock is colder than the rest of the house," she said. "The clock's door often springs open for no reason—and I've even heard muted voices coming from it."

When I asked who she thought it might be, she looked at me and said, "I don't know, and I don't want to know."

Governor John Edward Jones and his family never got the chance to live in the mansion. This could be the reason his ghost is said to be in residence. Jones served as Nevada's governor for a little over a year, from January 1895 to April 1896. He died while in office in 1896. Apparently the ghostly governor has not heard of term limits; he's been seen slowly walking through the mansion as if in search of someone.

Ghost at the State Capitol

*I*n the spring of 1880, Nevada's State Capitol Building was barely ten years old. Residents of Carson City, and indeed the entire state, were most proud of the beautiful new building and of the ground it sat upon, with its lawn and many trees. Capitol Square was not only the location where state business was conducted; it was also a place where people enjoyed gathering.

According to an article in the May 14, 1880, issue of the *Carson Morning Appeal*, Capitol Square was haunted by a hardworking ghost who spent the wee hours of the morning pushing a lawn mower over the grass. Now that is civic pride. But the strange thing about the lawn mower was that although it was heard, it was never seen. Nor was the ghostly man who pushed it.

Haunted House in Carson City

*F*ormer owner of the Wine House Saloon in Carson City George Bryson had also served as that city's mayor before moving to Reno. Once he'd set up residence in the Biggest Little City, the well-liked Bryson was appointed as Reno Municipal Court judge in 1914.

Eight years later on St. Patrick's Day 1922, a reporter for the *Reno Gazette-Journal* asked Judge Bryson about ghosts. The judge, being the type of man who liked to expound on every subject, was soon telling the reporter that he'd never heard of a haunt in Virginia City.

> But there was a haunted house in Carson City in which I would not live. No one else would take a chance of shaking hands or conversing with the elusive, ethereal occupant of the place; and except for the ghost, the house was uninhabited for at least twenty-five years. It burned down finally about twenty-five years ago, and the ghost never came back.
>
> The house was located near the orphans' home and was known as the haunted house. I have forgotten the reason it was haunted, but it seems to me that a murder had been committed there. I went into the house several times—but always in the daytime—and there was nothing the matter with the place by daylight. Of course the ghost only walked at night, and I wasn't sufficiently interested in the place after sundown to call there.
>
> Several families had moved into the place, but after the neighbors had told them about the ghosts, they moved out.

He finished his tale by saying, "I think the house was equipped with old-fashioned wooden shutters, the kind that rattle when the wind blows."

Ghosts Walk at the Old Mint

Although Congress established Nevada's mint in 1863, the building wasn't completed until December 1869. President Ulysses S. Grant made the obvious choice and appointed Abe Curry, known as the father of Carson City, to serve as the mint's superintendent.

Two years later, on February 11, 1871, the first seated liberty dollars with the CC (Carson City) mark were minted. Today these coins are rare. To put things into perspective, one of these dollars in uncirculated condition is now worth over $150,000. Check your coin jar carefully; even a Carson City seated liberty dollar in poor condition is worth more than $3,000.

But our story is not about numismatic values; it concerns the ghostly Osborne Parker, who is one of two ghostly residents of the old mint. Parker bears the distinction of being the only person to die at the mint during its operation. The unfortunate Mr. Parker was the victim of a terrible accident that happened less than two weeks from Christmas on December 12, 1872. A cold clear night in Carson City, all was quiet in the capital city. A full moon was just two days away.

A typical night, there was no indication of the tragedy that was about to occur as Osborne Parker went about his nightly routine in the basement of the mint. Suddenly, without warning, his sweater got caught and became entangled in the equipment. As he desperately tried to free himself, Osborne Parker was crushed to death, his pitiful cries for help echoing through the building.

And for a long time, no one wanted to work alone in the basement after Parker's hideous death. Some claimed that his anguished cries could be heard at the exact time of his death.

After producing about $50 million worth of coins (face value), the mint was closed in 1893, and the building was purchased by the state of Nevada in 1939 for use as a museum. The Nevada State Museum opened in the old mint in 1941. And of course there are the ghosts who are known to wander the premises. The ghostly Osborne Parker turns lights on and off and moves items around. He's here, and he wants everyone to know it. Just to make sure of that, the ghost is always accompanied by an icy draft. Those who've worked in the building after hours say they've heard Parker's footsteps coming up and down the stairs. Another favorite of his is the elevator, which some say runs on its own accord. He is also said to be responsible for the long low moans that have been known to echo through the building during the long winter months.

Not to be outdone is the ghostly Abe Curry, father of Carson City. Curry, who died suddenly a year after Osborne Parker, took his mint superintendent job seriously. Over 150 years later, he still does. The ghostly Curry wanders through the museum making sure everything is as it should be.

Some visitors to the museum claim to have seen Abe Curry in different areas of the building. They describe him as a stern-looking old man who seems happy with his surroundings. He frightens no one. That is not his intention; he is part of the museum, and apparently he intends to be so for a long time to come.

Abe Curry House

*G*hosts wander. And apparently Abe Curry does. He returns to the home he built at 406 North Nevada Street just two years before his death. His death left his family with few resources other than the house. Local lore says the Currys were so poor they couldn't even afford a decent headstone for Abe's grave. A century would pass before he received a headstone at the Lone Mountain Cemetery. The ghostly Abe Curry is believed to return to his former home hoping to check up on his wife and family, which tells us they didn't reunite in the afterlife.

The Abe Curry house was put on the National Register of Historic Places in 1987, and you are free to gaze at the house all you want—from the sidewalk. Please know that the house is a private residence. Dozens of people have seen the ghostly Curry, looking just as he did in life, wandering through the house.

Duane L. Bliss Loves His Home

German engineer Philip Deidesheimer developed square-set timbering in 1860 for the Ophir Mine in Virginia City, making for safer and more reliable mining. Every mining company saw the value of Deidesheimer's honeycomb system, and the demand for lumber in Virginia City increased significantly.

Seeing opportunity, Duane L. Bliss moved his family from Gold Hill to Carson City and invested in timberland around Lake Tahoe—a wise move. Bliss became wealthy by selling lumber from the area to mines in Virginia City. In 1879, he built his mansion across the street from the location of Nevada's future Governor's Mansion. Of course, Bliss had no way of knowing this when his fifteen-room, 8,500-square-foot, three-story home with seven marble fireplaces was built on the corner of West Mountain and North Robinson Streets.

It was a big beautiful mansion, the finest in Carson City, but there was a problem. Bliss had selected the site of a cemetery to build upon. The problem was solved with the bodies being moved to other locations. But we know that disturbing graves can cause hauntings and other issues. There is no word on whether or not Duane L. Bliss and his family were haunted by those who'd been forced to other locations. I bet they were.

What we do know is that Bliss Mansion is haunted. A lovely lady in a white flowing gown is one of the ghosts said to be roaming the mansion, but the ghost most often seen and felt is none other than Duane L. Bliss himself. He loved his home and apparently is quite comfortable here. You might feel a sudden icy chill or catch a glimpse of him on the staircase or in the backyard. Don't ask; he isn't ready to leave.

Little Jennie Clemens

*N*evadans, especially those who live in Northern Nevada, are very proud to tell you that Mark Twain, aka Samuel Clemens, got his writing start at the *Territorial Enterprise* in Virginia City, right here in Nevada. While his literary career was blossoming, Twain's brother, Orion Clemens, was involved in politics in Carson City as Nevada's first secretary of state. Helping Orion entertain guests at the small family home on North Division Street were his wife Mollie and daughter Jennie, the apple of her uncle Samuel's eye. When he visited his family, Mark Twain, the indulgent uncle, usually finished the evening by reading Jennie a bedtime story.

While she was taking donations to buy a Bible for her church, Jennie contracted spotted fever. The child's condition worsened, and with her worried family gathered at her bedside, Jennie Clemens died on February 1, 1864. She was nine years old. Her parents and her uncle Samuel were devastated. None of them would ever be the same. And within a few short years, Orion and Mollie Clemens left Nevada, never to return. Mark Twain would leave and return only twice.

This left no family members to care for little Jennie's gravesite. And this may be why Jennie Clemens wanders the Lone Mountain Cemetery in Carson City at all hours of the day and night. Those who've seen the glowing little specter say she is playing with other children and enjoying herself. Occasionally Jennie strikes out alone and makes her way to her former home on North Division Street a few blocks away. Over the years, she's been seen in the window of the upstairs bedroom where she died.

The Man in Black

September 28, 1879: a pleasant night with a full moon high in the sky. John was on his way home after a long day's work. He was less than a mile from the state prison in Carson City when he came upon a man dressed in black from head to toe.

The two were only about five feet apart, and John could clearly see that there was no kindness in this stranger's eyes, and there was something in the way the man stared at him.

Thinking he was about to be robbed, John asked, "What is it you want, stranger?"

Without a word, the man reached for his hip pocket. But John was faster. He pulled his pistol and fired five times. The bullets had no effect on the stranger. He remained standing.

"What on earth?" John asked.

Moving closer to the stranger, he reached for him. Just as he did so, the man disappeared. John waited, hoping the man would reappear. When he failed to do so, John walked on to his home. Try as he might, he couldn't get the stranger in black and his sudden disappearance out of his mind. He wasn't crazy. He knew what he'd seen. And he also knew that no earthly man could take five bullets and remain upright.

The next night he brought a friend with him, hoping that the stranger might reappear. He got his wish. At the same time that John had encountered him the previous night, the man in black appeared.

"Who are you and what do you want with John?" the friend asked.

The stranger glared at the two men and didn't say a word.

"Let's grab him!" John said.

And the two men ran toward the stranger. Later when telling their story, they would say that every time they reached for him, it was like trying to grab a handful of smoke. Because the two men were well thought of in the area, no one doubted the veracity of their story. But neither did anyone go looking for the ghostly man in black.

Does the Ghostly John Murphy Still Walk?

*J*ohn Murphy was hanged at the foot of Lone Mountain in Carson City on December 29, 1874, for the murder of John McCallum. As he stood on the gallows, he didn't deny his guilt, nor was he remorseful. Murphy was a Spiritualist who believed he would return as a ghost to walk the streets of Carson City once more.

While addressing the crowd that had come to see his execution, Murphy said, "I'll come back if I can. When you hear them chains rattling, look out for me."

On cold and rainy nights, a hunched elderly man is sometimes seen walking along Carson Street, his collar pulled up as if to ward off the cold. Listen! He is accompanied by the sound of rattling chains. Is this the ghostly John Murphy? Has he kept his promise? Has he returned to show that it is indeed possible to do so? Keep your distance. He was not a nice person in life. And it's doubtful being a ghost has improved his disposition any.

The Gardnerville Hotel and the Stagecoach Robbing Ghost

In the telling of ghost stories, history gets mixed up with lore. The story of the Kent House in Genoa is one such tale. The abandoned Kent House on the road between Genoa and Walley's Hot Springs was rumored to be haunted by the ghost of a stagecoach robber who'd died nearby. This is plausible since robberies did occur in this area. But stagecoach robbers generally got away with the goods. Occasionally one might be arrested and sent to prison. But rarely did he meet resistance and a bullet, ending his life and his chosen career.

The stagecoach robber ghost could have been a man who died with his boots on—that is, he died of old age rather than having his life cut short by some lawman. Perhaps he was just a teller of tall tales who liked to boast of his misspent youth.

No matter how he died, the ghost at the Kent House probably wasn't a very happy ghost. He was said to have made things miserable for those who'd lived at the Kent House, with all manner of strange noises and cold breezes. His apparition may have even made an appearance or two before startled guests. When a place is said to be haunted over time, it's a safe bet that someone has had encounters with a ghost.

But Lawrence Gilman was not the type to be afraid of ghosts. In 1873 he married Mary Singleton, the widow of J. T. Singleton, and in 1879 they became the owners of the Kent House. Gilman knew exactly where he wanted the old hotel placed. But Mary Gilman was not impressed. She did not like the new area and would not live there with her husband. She chose to stay in Genoa—and divorce her husband.

And in the spring of 1881, Gilman had the Kent House taken apart and hauled piece by piece from Genoa to the seven-acre tract of land he'd recently purchased from his friends John and Mary Gardner, early settlers to the region. Mary Gilman was probably surprised when her ex-husband proved to be a visionary. Soon other buildings and businesses would be erected in this area eight miles south of Genoa. It would be called Gardnerville in honor of John Gardner.

Lawrence Gilman's Kent House was renamed the Gardnerville Hotel; it would serve travelers in the region for many years to come. Those who knew about the former Kent House assured themselves that the ghostly stagecoach robber had stayed behind in a copse of cottonwood trees near the spot where the old hotel had once stood. He may be there still.

The Ghost at Saarman's Ranch

*T*he elderly Mr. and Mrs. Saarman lived in a small house on a rented ranch near Gardnerville in the Carson Valley. A hardworking couple, they were well liked in this small farming community where everyone knew everyone else. One day was much as any other day; most folks occupied themselves with their crops and their animals, and the weather—until tragedy struck at the Saarmans' home.

May 15, 1895. Later, Mr. Saarman would say that he was working in the fields around four in the afternoon when he happened to look up and notice smoke coming from his house. What on earth, he wondered. There was no time to think. He dropped his tools and raced to his house. There he was faced with a horrendous sight; his wife's lifeless body lay in the kitchen. She'd been hacked to death with a hatchet, and her body was partially burned.

Four hours would pass before Mr. Saarman notified neighbors of the terrible incident. What had he done in those four hours between the time he discovered Mrs. Saarman's body and the time he'd informed people? That was the question on everyone's mind. When asked about it, Mr. Saarman, who did not have a good command of the English language, claimed he had been so distressed at the gruesome murder that he carried on his daily chores—unhitched the horse, milked the cows, and fed the chickens—before telling anyone about his wife.

The cold-blooded killing of an elderly woman was not going to go unpunished here in the Carson Valley. A $200 reward for the arrest and conviction of the killer was offered. The Douglas County Commission added $500 to the reward, and it was assumed that the state would add yet another $500 as well.

On the belief that a homeless man was responsible for killing Mrs. Saarman, authorities rounded up two homeless men on June 1. But after an hour-long interrogation, and with no evidence to hold them, the sheriff, fearing a lynch mob, took the men out of the county and released them. The case was no closer to being solved.

Six months after her murder, Mrs. Saarman returned to her home. And night after night, the ghost of the slain woman appeared in the kitchen, silently trying to wipe away bloodstains that remained on the kitchen floor. Frightened of the ghost, the cook was the first to leave the house. Two family members fled the house next. No one wanted to stay there. Eager to get to the bottom of the ghostly appearance, a man offered twenty dollars to anyone who would spend the night in the Saarman house. No one was brave enough to take him up on his generous offer.

February 8, 1898. Three years later, facts came out that changed the course of the investigation. Apparently Mrs. Saarman had been a miser with a large amount of gold she kept hidden away from her husband, who also happened to be the beneficiary of a $2,700 life insurance policy. Suspicion fell back on the widower. Judge Mack ordered the grand jury in Genoa to conduct a thorough investigation of the murder.

After all, there were no witnesses other than Mr. Saarman. And there was still that question of the four hours that had lapsed between the time he'd discovered his wife's body and the time he'd notified anyone. Just when it looked as if Mr. Saarman was going to jail on a charge of murder, early-day science was put forth, and it saved the day for Mr. Saarman. The February 19, 1898, issue of the *Carson Daily Appeal* carried the following article:

> The Saarman Case: Dr. Young publishes a card in the *Genoa Courier* to the effect that Mr. Saarman did not kill his wife as the post mortem examination showed a criminal assault before the killing.

"Criminal assault" was an early-day euphemism for rape. This proved Mr. Saarman's innocence, but sadly the guilty person was never caught.

Today the old house is long gone. But don't you wonder—does the ghostly Mrs. Saarman still come and try to wipe away the bloodstains of her terrible murder that went unsolved all those years ago?

A Ghost at the American Laundry

*W*as there really a ghost? Or was this ghost story merely created as a way to get off work early? We can't blame the tale on the influences of a full moon; a crescent moon hung in the sky the night the ghost story first appeared in the *Carson Daily Appeal* on May 27, 1886. The newspaper reported the following:

Was It a Ghost? An Apparition Stalks through the American Laundry

For some days past there have been queer rumors of a ghost seen in the American Laundry, run by Mr. Millard. An *Appeal* reporter investigated the report yesterday. As the story goes at 8 o'clock last Thursday the hands were sitting in the laundry, having just knocked off work, when a woman quite richly dressed and a stranger to everyone walked into the laundry. She said nothing as she went past the group, but proceeded to the engine room where she opened the furnace door and looked in. This act rather puzzled those present as they all wondered what the woman wanted of the furnace and one of the group rose and went toward her to see what she wanted. He bowed but she swept passed him without a word and made toward the door. He followed close behind and called to her. When she reached the door, she vanished, but the man who followed her vows that she did not go down the steps, but simply disappeared.

Elder Millard was coming up the lane, and was asked if he had met anyone coming down, but he said no.

Mrs. Millard was in the yard and says that no one came down the steps. The hands quite excited rushed about the premises in search of the strange woman, but could find no trace of her. They claim that a live woman could not have passed out of the building and into the yard without being seen, and as no one saw her after she reached the door, all unite in pronouncing her a genuine ghost.

Ghost Bride of Ferris Mansion

Though far away, I will chase you with murky
brands and, when chill death has severed soul and
body, everywhere my shade shall haunt you.

—*Virgil*, The Aeneid

*I*f you should walk past this old Victorian at 311 West Third Street
in Carson City on a warm summer day, you might tell yourself
that this house isn't haunted. After all, historians point out that the
Ferris Mansion is the boyhood home of George Washington Gale
Ferris Jr., who designed and created the Ferris wheel for the World's
Columbian Exposition in 1893.

Ferris had lived in Nevada from an early age. He was five years
old when his father, George Washington Gale Ferris Sr., moved the
family from Illinois to Nevada. In 1868, the Ferris family moved into
the home on West Third Street where they would live for the next
twelve years.

The ghost bride story is the best-known tale connected to the
Ferris mansion. The Ferris family was not the first to live in the mansion, and many other families have lived there since they did, so
chances are she isn't connected to them. But who is she?

My favorite version of the tale has the ghostly bride appearing at
a long-ago wedding with guests wondering who the other bride was.
Smiling happily, she stood beside the bride and groom and vanished
before they'd completed their vows. A woman who encountered the
crying bride on a tour a few years ago was shocked to realize she'd
been talking with a ghost.

> I felt so sorry for her; she looked so pitiful in her old
> fashioned bridal gown.

"Listen," I said, trying to comfort her, "I've been married three times, and I can assure you that life has a way of working these things out."

That's when she began sobbing that her beloved groom had deserted her at the altar—then she turned from me and walked right through the wall.

Aside from the ghostly bride, there have been incidents of disembodied voices singing loudly in the mansion at all hours of the day and night. Then there is the aroma of strong aftershave that wafts through the house on certain nights.

George Washington Gale Jr. died unexpectedly at the age of thirty-seven. Unless he is the ghostly man with the aftershave, or one of the disembodied singers, he has not made a ghostly appearance here on West Third Street. Is the Ferris Mansion haunted? Some may tell you there are no ghosts in residence. Others who've witnessed ghostly activity will certainly have a different story to tell.

Rinckel Mansion

*H*ere's a bit of ghostly irony for you. The 1942 film *The Remarkable Andrew* was filmed here at Rinckel Mansion in Carson City. The plot of the film involves the ghostly Andrew Jackson, the seventh president of the United States. What better place to film a movie about a ghost than a haunted house?

The Rinckel Mansion has been listed on the National Register of Historic Places since 1975. Located at 102 North Curry Street in Carson City, the mansion was built between 1874 and 1876 by wealthy businessman Mathias Rinckel. The Rinckels' first child, Louise, was born in the house a short time later. Louise is the star of our story, for she is the resident ghost.

Although she was attractive and received much attention from well-intentioned suitors, Louise was content to live her life unmarried. She would be the last Rinckel to live in the house. She died in the very room she'd been born in. And that created a problem for other owners. Louise had been a teetotaler in life who despised alcohol. A happy day for Louise was the day the Eighteenth Amendment and the Volstead Act, outlawing alcohol, were passed.

The Carlson House was a restaurant that moved into the Rinckel Mansion and converted Louise's bedroom into a bar, complete with big-screen TV. I remember that the popular restaurant served excellent fried pickles and a good Bloody Mary. But the ghostly Louise was not pleased with the situation. Although Louise never chose to appear, she would often topple liquor bottles, knock over drinks, break empty glasses, and send a chilly air whooshing through the bar area. If that didn't get people's attention, the ghostly Louise would turn the lights off and on and unplug the TV.

Eventually the Carlson House closed, and the building was purchased by the Nevada Press Foundation. And, lucky for those who were interested in attempting to communicate with Louise

Rinckel on the other side, the building was available to rent for parties and other special events. Recently a new owner purchased the Rinckel Mansion with plans to convert it to a tea room and bed-and-breakfast. This seems like a wonderful opportunity to spend some quality time at a historic Victorian mansion. And if you visit, please remember not to propose a toast if you should encounter the ghostly Louise.

Nevada State Prison

*T*here's no question the old Nevada State Prison is haunted. How could it be otherwise? The prison was established in 1862 at the site of Abe Curry's Warm Springs Hotel in Carson City. Once Nevada achieved statehood in 1864, the prison was built, and Abe Curry, aka the father of Carson City, became its first warden. In the late 1870s, the prison gained attention with the discovery of fossilized footprints of prehistoric creatures.

The footprints were found to be La Brea fauna of the Pliocene epoch. And there was much debate among scientists over just what creature the footprints belonged to. By the mid-1900s, scientists generally agreed that the footprints were those of giant sloths. But other ancient creatures roamed this area as well: deer, elk, big-toothed cats, wooly mammoths, and horses were among them. Granted there are ghostly horses, cats, and dogs, but it's highly unlikely that any of these ancient animals are among those haunting the prison.

The complex would serve as a maximum security prison until 1989. And on May 12, 2012, the facility was closed down as a prison; shortly thereafter it opened for tours.

If you doubt there are ghosts lingering here, you might want to take one of the ghost walks or tours offered at the prison. Even those who don't believe in things that go bump in the night will find a tour intriguing.

Heading it all up is Susan Bernard and her group, Nevada State Prison Paranormal. Susan has a special connection to the prison; a relative of her husband Jim served as warden there. If anyone knows the history and the ghosts here, it is Susan. During a recent conversation, she told me about some of those who've stayed behind here. One she calls "Dark" follows her throughout the old facility. She is not fearful of him and believes him to be a former inmate who was executed here. Ghosts become territorial of their chosen location, as some ghost hunters have found out while investigating the prison.

Susan and Nevada State Prison Paranormal have gained acceptance with the ghostly residents, but once in a while an investigator will find that they are not liked by the ghosts.

Ghostly Soldiers

*F*ort Churchill in Silver Springs has been a Nevada historic state park since 1957. The establishment of Fort Churchill in 1861 began with an incident that took place in 1860 at Williams Station, a Pony Express stop in the Carson Valley. In the spring of 1860, two young Paiute women were kidnapped, raped, and held captive at Williams Station. One of the women escaped to tell her people what had happened at the station. Wanting revenge, Paiute warriors attacked the station, setting it afire and killing three men.

Fearing that this marked the beginning of renewed conflict with the Native Americans, William Ormsby gathered a militia group and led them toward Pyramid Lake to squelch the uprising. The Paiutes, led by Chief Numaga, were familiar with the land and easily out-maneuvered the untrained volunteers. Seventy-six men, including Major Ormsby, were killed during the skirmish that would become known as the Battle of Pyramid Lake. The US government estab-lished Fort Churchill at present-day Silver Springs in order to stop further conflicts. At any given time, there were at least two hundred men serving at Fort Churchill.

Five years after Nevada attained statehood, the US government abandoned Fort Churchill in 1869, and the land and buildings were sold to Samuel Buckland for $750. Here he built a fine home for his family, known today as Buckland Station. Fifteen years later, the remains of soldiers were moved from Fort Churchill Cemetery to either the Presidio in San Francisco or the Lone Mountain Cemetery in Carson City. Forty-four would be reburied at the latter site, leav-ing only the graves of Samuel and Eliza Buckland and family in the Fort Churchill Cemetery.

And here again is yet another incident of graves being disturbed. It's not surprising that the area of the Lone Mountain Cemetery near the soldier memorial is thought to be one of the more haunted areas of the region. The ghostly soldier who roams the cemetery after dark is thought to be one of those whose remains were moved from Fort Churchill Cemetery. There is such an air of sadness about him that many who have seen him are so overcome with emotion that they break down sobbing.

Over at Fort Churchill, there is nothing left of the old fort. The adobe ruins that are often shown in photos of the fort were actually created in the 1930s. No, there is nothing left but the two ghostly soldiers who are said to roam the area. Thought to be two enlisted men who contracted fever and died here, they are usually seen on the darkest of nights. These ghosts are believed to be residual hauntings, as there is no interaction between them and those who've encountered them.

Yerington

*Y*erington is a tiny town of about three thousand people—and a couple of ghosts. Wovoka (Jack Wilson), the Paiute religious leader and creator of the ghost dance that led to the Wounded Knee tragedy, was born here, as was mystery writer Nevada Barr.

According to local lore, a ghost resides in the Lyon County Courthouse. The courthouse was designed by noted Nevada architect Frederic DeLongchamps in 1911 after a bitter battle with the neighboring town of Dayton. Dayton was the seat of Lyon County and promised to build another courthouse after theirs burned down. Things change, especially here in Nevada. Before Dayton could follow through with their plans, Yerington was given the county seat, and the new courthouse was ready for business in the spring of 1912.

The ghost here at the courthouse is said to be that of a former inmate of the old jail. As with many old courthouses, the jail was inside the building. This particular man wanted out of jail one way or the other. Sadly, he chose to hang himself in his cell one night as a means of escape. That wasn't a good solution to his problem. It's been many decades, and he is still here in the building, moaning and crying and walking the halls when most of those who work here have gone for the day. It doesn't rain often here, but when it does, the ghost seems to be the most active. Some claim he has even tapped them on the shoulder—this could be his way of reminding them that he is still incarcerated here, and may be for a very long time.

The Kelsay House in Fish Springs

*T*he house that came to be known as the Kelsay House was built in Virginia City and was later moved to Carson City. The segment about the ghosts who were haunting a house in Fish Springs caused a sensation when it aired on the January 23, 1991, episode of the TV show *Unsolved Mysteries.* In the show, the Kelsays told their harrowing story of their encounters with a ghost they called Samuel. As verification of their story, they presented a photo and negative of the ghost, which was taken in 1982.

The Kelsays bought the house in 1978 and had it moved to land that was owned by Mrs. Kelsay's family in Fish Springs. Ghost researchers know that remodeling can cause ghost activity to increase. Apparently the ghost didn't like his residence being relocated. It wasn't long after the move that the family realized they were not alone in the home. Things were being moved from one room to the other, footsteps and strange noises echoed through the house, and the thermostat was being turned up to ninety-five degrees. In desperation, the family turned to a psychic friend who told them that the ghost was named Samuel and had been attached to the house for a long time, at least since it had stood in Virginia City.

As has been seen in the past, ghosts apparently pick and choose who they will interact with. Other families that had lived in the house didn't have any ghostly encounters. But the psychic believed that Samuel was there because he felt a connection to one of the daughters and wanted to protect her. Perhaps she reminded him of someone he'd known in life.

All the ghost activity, the disembodied noises, Samuel's appearances in a photo Mrs. Kelsay had taken of one of her children—it was all too much for the Kelsays. They eventually sold the house and moved away.

Central Nevada

The Lady in Red Ghost at the Mizpah Hotel

The beautiful Lady in Red is the most famous ghost at the Mizpah Hotel. She has been encountered by numerous guests over the years. In the late 1990s, just before the hotel was closed up, my family and I were in Tonopah and staying at the Mizpah Hotel. We'd come with the express purpose of meeting up with the Lady in Red ghost.

Legend has it that long ago a young prostitute was murdered outside her room on the fifth floor. Naturally we wanted rooms on that floor. After dinner, we took a stroll through the downtown area and then took our post with our cameras up on the fifth floor. If the ghost made an appearance, we would be ready for her. As we waited, the elevator continuously went from one floor to the next, always stopping at the fifth floor—and always empty. It was nearing three in the morning; a chill fell across the hallway. I yawned, setting off a string of yawning. Apparently the Lady in Red wasn't going to make an appearance.

"I'm tired," I said. "And I'm not waiting for this ghost anymore."

Yes, everyone agreed. Let's call it a night. No sooner had we decided to end our vigil than she appeared. She wasn't the beautiful Lady in Red, but rather a greenish-blue glowing woman that floated from one end of the hall to the other, finally vanishing into the wall.

We'd seen her! But not a one of us had had the presence of mind to get a photograph. When any of us share this story, we realize that there will be that demand for proof. All I'll say about that is some things just can't be proven. This is one of them.

Years later, my late friend Robert Allen also had an encounter with the Lady in Red ghost. Robert was an entertainer and the creator of the Las Vegas Ghost Tour. When he wasn't busy at that or a number of other businesses, Robert and his wife Deborah traveled the world. And in his spare time he occasionally took part in ghost hunts.

One mid-December, Robert and I joined forces in Goldfield to visit Virginia Ridgway and to investigate the Goldfield Hotel. The investigation was uneventful, unless you want to count cold spots at various locations throughout the old hotel. When we called it a night, Bill and I headed home, and Robert and his friend Richard headed to Tonopah. There they spent the night at the Mizpah Hotel.

Hoping for an encounter with the Lady in Red ghost, Robert stayed in room 304. He was never sure just who the ghost was, but he was certain that when he woke from a sound sleep, someone not of this world was standing over him.

"Okay, Lady in Red, what do you want?" he asked.

There was no response. He waited. The day had been long and exhausting, so he rolled over and went back to sleep. Later he admitted that he thought it was the Lady in Red checking him out. The next morning after breakfast, Richard and Robert went up to room 502, which is the Lady in Red's room. The plan was to shoot some video. They discussed the lighting and, yes, the Lady herself. And as they talked about her and who she might have been, the dresser's top drawer slid open noisily.

Startled, they looked at each other. Neither said a word. The dresser was across the room from them. "Are you here, Lady in Red?" Robert asked. "Would you like to make an appearance in our video?"

Realizing it was a silly question to ask a ghost, Robert explained that he only wanted to let her know why they were there. It may have been her rattling that drawer, or one of the other ghosts who haunt the Mizpah—who can say?

Strange Lady on the Elevator

*W*hat happens when something you've always denied the existence of suddenly causes you to rethink your beliefs? The man who shared this ghostly experience with me would never admit that his experience had anything to do with a ghost. He'd lived most of his life in Tonopah and has recently passed on. He was a brilliant man who willingly shared his story, but he didn't want his name associated with it.

"I don't want folks thinking I'm crazy," he said and then added, "I can't explain what happened—but I will tell you I still don't believe in ghosts." Be that as it may, this was his story:

> It was sometime in the early 1980s, and a local men's club was holding its luncheon meeting at the Mizpah Hotel. When the meeting concluded, some of the men wandered through the hotel, and others found their way to the bar. I didn't drink, so I started looking around the different floors of the hotel.
>
> After I looked around the second floor, I decided I'd seen enough and hopped in the elevator. As the doors closed, I hit the button for the lobby. But the elevator started going up. I punched the button again and again. But the elevator kept going up.
>
> The elevator stopped on the fifth floor, and an attractive lady stepped in. She gave me a nod and a smile. I pressed the down button for the lobby and chatted with her during the elevator's descent. When the elevator arrived at the lobby, the door opened and I gallantly stepped aside for her to walk out ahead of me. I was shocked to realize that no one was in the elevator with me. Where had the lady gone? I wondered.

I stepped out of the elevator thinking I must have a drink, even though I am a teetotaler. I hurried to the bar and asked the bartender for a double anything. Then turning toward the five men at the bar, I told them about my unusual experience in the elevator.

One of my friends asked if I talked with her.

"I was the one doing the talking. She merely smiled and nodded," I told him. "There was something strange about that lady."

The bartender placed my double in front of me, and I quickly gulped it down.

"What was the lady wearing?" someone asked me.

"I'm not much on ladies' fashion, but she seemed to be wearing some sort of a red dress," I said.

The man smiled at me. "Son, you've just been in the elevator with our Lady in Red ghost who resides on the fifth floor."

I ordered a refill and chugged that down as well. I left the hotel, not wanting any further involvement with her or any other ghosts.

Those Pesky Kids on the Fourth Floor

*H*ousekeepers at the Mizpah Hotel tell of ghostly children who run through the halls laughing and screaming. Of special annoyance is when these pesky kids pull clean towels from their racks and jump up and down on freshly made beds. A former employee admitted that she hadn't believed a word of the stories involving ghost kids when she came to work at the Mizpah.

Excuses for sloppy housekeeping and bed making, she told herself. And she was convinced of this. Until that morning on the fourth floor when she finished making a bed nicely and neatly, only to have it destroyed by two ghostly little boys who climbed upon the bed and began jumping up and down on it.

"I couldn't believe my eyes. Leastwise, I didn't *want* to believe my eyes," she said. "I was too scared to even speak. I left the room thinking I'd come back and fix it later. Instead, I quit that day—I don't want anything to do with ghosts."

They may be nuisances, but these little ghosts are enjoying spending time at the Mizpah. Employees know all about them and their antics. Some housekeepers have even implored the pesky kids to please not mess up their work. Guests don't seem to mind and have reported seeing them happily chasing each other down the hallway.

Politician in the Bathtub

*W*hen you research and write about ghosts, you're always look-ing for that one good reason that will explain why a place is haunted. This story first came to my attention in an old book called *Green Felt Jungle*. Authors Ed Reid and Ovid Demaris presented an interesting, if jarring, exposé of 1950s–1960s Las Vegas gambling and the mob's involvement. Included in the book is the tale of US sena-tor Key Pittman's 1940 death and how it was covered up so that he would win an election.

This was achieved, according to the story, by keeping Pittman's body on ice in a bathtub at the Mizpah Hotel until after he'd been reelected. While many Nevada historians hotly deny the tale, you've got to admit that this could well be the reason Key Pittman haunts the Mizpah Hotel. How do I know he does? I've had two people, who knew nothing of the bathtub story, tell me of seeing his ghost. During a family stay at the hotel, my daughter-in-law Peggy had an encounter with the ghostly Pittman. He wasn't in the bathtub but lurked over her bed most of the night.

"He was looking sad and sickly," she said. "I told him to leave me alone, and he only stared at me."

When we got home, I showed Peggy a photo of Key Pittman, and she nodded. "This is him. But he was older and not as healthy look-ing when he hovered over the bed."

Years later, a friend I'll call Sarah and I were staying at the Miz-pah for a conference. We were both exhausted from the long drive and drew straws to see who would get the bathroom first. Sarah won. Smiling, she gathered her things and went to take what she said would be a long leisurely bubble bath.

No sooner was the water flowing than she came running from the bathroom. "There's an old man in the bathtub—I can see right through him. He's a ghost!"

There was nobody in the tub when I went in to check. But later, as I'd done with Peggy, I showed her a photo of Key Pittman, and she gasped, "That's him! That's the man in the bathtub."

These two incidents lead me to believe there is some truth to the body on ice story. When I used this argument with a historian, he told me the official story of Key Pittman's death. After being rushed from the Riverside Hotel to the Washoe County Hospital, Pittman died of a massive heart attack. Admittedly, it sounds almost logical. The historian then stressed that since Key Pittman loved the Mizpah and often hung out there, he might choose to haunt a favorite spot. And that is possible—but I doubt it.

Goldfield Hotel

*A*t this writing, the Goldfield Hotel is for sale, along with a few other properties, for $4.9 million. It is anyone's guess whether or not someone will buy the old building and if it will ever reopen for business.

The first time I investigated the Goldfield Hotel was the summer of 2001 when Bill and I were invited to come to Goldfield and take part in one of Fox's *Scariest Places on Earth* episodes. During our visit, we met two fascinating people who would remain our friends for the next twenty years: the late Virginia Ridgway, who was the Goldfield historian and caretaker of the Goldfield Hotel, and the late Bryan Smalley, who was an Esmeralda deputy sheriff at the time. Both Virginia and Bryan loved their town and its spooky hotel.

The more gregarious of the two, Virginia was always happy to welcome more ghost investigations, which equaled more publicity for the hotel and the town, which sits in the middle of nowhere, halfway between Reno and Las Vegas.

It didn't take me long to realize that there was something definitely special about the Goldfield Hotel, in a paranormal sort of way. Even as we were rushed through the building, the feeling was palpable. The director was concerned only with getting another show in the can and hurried us through the hotel, one floor after another.

Shooting completed, Bill drove us across the desert through the early morning darkness, both of us realizing that we'd be back to the Goldfield Hotel again.

Midnight Ride with Bryan

Bryan Smalley was an Esmeralda County deputy sheriff when I first met him in the early 2000s through Virginia Ridgway. A lover of Central Nevada history and its gems, Bryan didn't necessarily believe or disbelieve in ghosts. But out of kindness he agreed to show me some of what was *supposed* to be the Goldfield area's most haunted locations. This involved a ride-along as Bryan was working the graveyard shift. I signed the waivers and slid into the passenger seat of the deputy's car.

First stop was the location where Virgil Earp died in 1906 of pneumonia. It was after midnight, and no one was out and about in this town of roughly three hundred.

"Virginia tells me his ghost is sometimes seen here," I said, squinting out at the darkness.

"That's what they say," Bryan said, waiting a moment for any ghostly activity.

On this night, the ghostly Virgil Earp didn't make an appearance. He was probably too busy haunting the O.K. Corral in Tombstone, Arizona.

At the Goldfield Cemetery, Bryan explained that in 1906 Goldfield had actually moved its cemetery to accommodate those coming from across the country for the Gans-Nelson fight.

"That fight went forty-two rounds," Bryan said as I scanned the cemetery for any ghostly action.

Seeing nothing, I asked about ghosts.

"If there's a ghost here, it's little Joy," Bryan said. "Her family couldn't afford a headstone, so her mother stole a stone from the Sundog School and carved one herself."

"Virginia told me that a Russian count is buried here too."

"Count Podhorski. Yes, he was murdered by his girlfriend's husband."

Later, Bryan drove us to a spot where pioneers coming westward were buried. No headstones mark the location, and it truly is in the middle of nowhere.

"Virginia has seen the ghost of a little blonde girl here," he said.

I looked and—there was movement off in the distance.

"Do you see that?" I asked, hoping the little blonde girl had decided to make an appearance.

"It's a mountain lion," Bryan said.

I looked at him. Was he kidding or not? I couldn't tell. "I guess we aren't getting out of the car," I said.

"Nope," he replied.

To this day I'm still not sure if he was kidding me or not.

Back on the highway, one traffic stop—a speeder who didn't realize this is about the worst place to speed in Nevada. I now have the experience. And I can tell you, it feels very different on this side of a traffic ticket.

It was nearing four, and Bryan drove me back to the Santa Fe Motel with more information than I'd started out with. As I told Bill about the night, I made a promise to myself to begin researching Count Podhorski and little Joy the following day.

Little Joy Fleming

If you should visit the Goldfield Cemetery one night and happen to see a child happily scampering among the Joshua trees and the headstones, you've encountered little Joy. Joy died here in Goldfield of diphtheria in 1907. Her heartbroken parents were so poor that they couldn't even afford a headstone to mark the child's last resting place.

Joy's mother did what she had to do. That night, while most of Goldfield slept, she made her way to the Sundog School, pulling an old toy wagon behind her. She loaded a heavy stone block into the wagon and started for the cemetery. Once there, she placed the block on Joy's grave and spent the rest of the night chiseling the simple message "Joy" into the stone.

The story of the mother's love touched everyone who read about it. In the 1980s, after the headstone had stood there in the desert cemetery for more than seventy years, Nevada state employees replaced it with a new stone.

The Cowboy Ghost of the Goldfield Hotel

*V*irginia Ridgway, who served as caretaker for the hotel of more than thirty years, believed there were several ghosts in residence at the old Goldfield Hotel; one of them was a menacing cowboy ghost on the third floor. What's more, Virginia told of being lifted off the ground and shoved against the wall by this ghost numerous times. One afternoon, Virginia and an Esmeralda County sheriff's deputy (this may or may not have been Bryan Smalley; neither of them ever said) were on the third floor of the hotel when they noticed smoke at the end of the hall. As they stared at the smoke, it suddenly dissipated, and a tall man dressed in black from head to foot stood staring at them.

"Who are you?" Virginia asked. "Do you need any help?"

Rather than acknowledge them, the ghostly cowboy seemed to stare through them.

Whoever he was, this ghost seemed to be very angry. Virginia believed the cowboy was either Wyatt or Virgil Earp. However, after researching happenings at the Goldfield Hotel, she agreed with my conclusion that this ghost might be that of James P. "Curly" Fennell, who died of a gunshot wound in his room at the hotel on the morning of July 9, 1925. The official cause of death was suicide, but there were many unanswered questions concerning Fennell's death.

In his pocket was a $1,700 cashier's check he had planned to use in opening his business in Goldfield. Fennell also had information about a $30,000 Sparks bank robbery and was under subpoena to go back to Reno and testify about what he knew. There was also the fact that Mrs. Fennell changed her story concerning her husband's death. Did Curly Fennell take his own life or was he murdered? We will never know. And this might be one reason the cowboy ghost on the third floor is so angry.

Sorrowful Saga at the Goldfield

*V*irginia Ridgway was the caretaker for the Goldfield Hotel for more than thirty years. In that time, she experienced many ghostly encounters and shared them with the media and with friends old and new whenever she got the chance. Shortly before she relocated to Reno, Virginia told me of a tragic incident that had happened at the Goldfield Hotel. A young man in a black cowboy hat came to Goldfield from Texas to stand in front of the Goldfield Hotel. There is nothing unusual in this; thousands of ghost enthusiasts come to the hotel every year for such a selfie.

When he met up with her, Virginia said that he had told her and others that the ghosts of the hotel had demanded that he come to the hotel. No one thought much about it; people come to Goldfield with such stories all the time. No, no one gave the young man in the big black cowboy hat a second thought. Until the night he went to the steps in front of the Goldfield Hotel and shot himself to death. Virginia said he'd left a note stating that he'd been ordered by the ghosts of the Goldfield Hotel to kill himself.

"Once in a while after that, I'd see him there out front when I drove by," Virginia said. "It wasn't the cowboy ghost that lifted me and pushed me against the wall. It was that young man from Texas. I recognized him right away."

Séance in Elizabeth's Room

I've taken part in numerous séances at the Goldfield Hotel. While they might not offer up acceptable evidence, they are interesting and can at times offer information. A late fall afternoon, it will soon be dark. This is when the ghosts who reside in this hotel become most active. In the meantime, a group of ghost hunters decide that we should conduct another séance in room 109, Elizabeth's room. They've been done before. But maybe, just maybe, we will learn something new about Elizabeth.

The tragic Elizabeth is the most famous ghost here. There are two schools of thought about her. There are those who believe that such a young woman did indeed exist and that she was murdered here in room 109 to keep her pregnancy a secret. Then there are those who believe that Elizabeth is nothing more than legend based loosely on Mae Barrick, a young prostitute who made the mistake of falling in love with the cruel businessman George Wingfield.

But there could be other possibilities. Perhaps the ghostly Elizabeth is simply a ghost who happens to enjoy the attention and affection bestowed upon her by ghost enthusiasts. And so we sat on the floor, in the time-honored circle, knowing that ours would neither be the first séance conducted here at the Goldfield Hotel nor the last. We joined hands and called for Elizabeth. This is not a new way of trying to get in touch with the dead. Séances have been conducted since the early 1800s, and possibly long before that.

We ask for Elizabeth to join us. Silence. We ask for Elizabeth again. A medium in our group moans and drops his head to his chest. "I have come a long way to tell you about George Wingfield," he says.

"Who are you?" I ask.

"I am Elizabeth, and I want to tell you about George Wingfield."

"What about him?" a woman asks.

"He didn't kill me. He didn't even know me."

"Why are you here?" I ask.

"I have come to save the good name of George Wingfield."

"We know he wasn't a very nice person," someone says.

"Yes, but he did not kill me."

"Did you die in this room?" I ask.

"No."

"Were you held captive in this room?"

"No."

"Do you stay here at the Goldfield Hotel?"

"I visit on occasion."

"You said you came from far away. Where is that?"

The medium raises his head and opens his eyes. The séance is over. And the ghost who has joined us is gone.

Darkness has fallen across Goldfield. We gather our scientific equipment for a night of exploring. We are all hoping that the ghostly Elizabeth will rejoin us during the night.

Ghost Adventures and Me at the Goldfield Hotel

*T*here are numerous ghost stories associated with the old Goldfield Hotel. The place is very active, and you just never know what's going to happen there, especially when Zak Bagans is involved. For some reason, ghosts either love him or hate him.

When I got the call about appearing with Zak Bagans's *Ghost Adventures* "Return to Goldfield" episode, I was thrilled. I hadn't seen Zak in a while and was looking forward to catching up with him and the guys again—especially at the Goldfield, where we shared so many memories of past investigations.

As Bill and I drove to Tonopah, I thought of all the people I'd explored and investigated the Goldfield Hotel with over the years. Many of them had passed on.

"This is all so bittersweet," I sighed. "On the one hand it will be exhilarating to go into the old hotel again. On the other, it will be so sad."

This would be the first time I'd been to the Goldfield Hotel since the death of EVP experts Mark and Debby Constantino, and I couldn't help but remember the first time I brought them to the hotel. Ten years had passed since that night—it seemed like a hundred.

Bill and I met with Zak, the guys, and the camera crew and then caught up a bit. After being mic'd, I waited for Zak to start the action, and into the hotel we went. It was all the same, and yet it was different. Gone was the lobby desk; in its stead was a fake fireplace. The hotel seemed somehow cleaner and fresher, almost like it had been smudged. As we went further into the lobby, an overwhelming sense of sadness fell over me; I fought hard to hold back tears. Later a friend who watched the episode would say that Zak and I both seemed to be experiencing the same emotions. A heavy loss, coming to terms with the murder-suicide deaths of two people we'd counted as friends had not been quick or easy. There would always be the question: Why?

I sensed that Mark was with us almost from the moment we stepped through the door. And he was not alone. No, it wasn't Debby who accompanied him. He had been escorted here on this night for one reason, and that was to secure Zak's forgiveness for having killed Debby. I tried to see who was escorting him—I couldn't. Some sort of gatekeeper is the sense I was picking up on.

As an experiment, Zak had had every window in the hotel blacked out so that no light had entered days before the investigation. This may have drawn more negative ghosts. All I knew was that there were ghosts walking with us that night. They may have been long-dead friends or enemies, but they were there along with Mark Constantino.

On the fourth floor, Zak captured Mark's voice quite clearly. We tried to talk with him further but got no response. Perhaps it was an effort to let us know of his presence. The next night, Zak and the crew were able to get evidence of an unfriendly spirit that's been hanging out at the Goldfield Hotel for a very long time. And he doesn't like visitors. No doubt, he is responsible for a lot of the negative activity that's taken place at the old hotel throughout the years.

Who's Scarier, the Clowns or the Ghosts?

*I*f you happen to suffer from coulrophobia—that is, fear of clowns—this story is not for you. Tonopah's famous—or not-so-famous—Clown Motel is all about clowns. All those stuffed clowns and clown photos, everywhere you look—it's enough to make you want to break out your feather duster and get busy.

Let's be honest, the motel is not the Taj Mahal, nor does it pretend to be. But there is no denying that the Clown Motel, which bills itself as "America's Scariest Motel," is a unique place to spend the night—especially if you have a soft spot for clowns and ghosts.

Yes, somewhere along the way, ghosts have joined the clowns, and the motel is known for both. It seems like the perfect place for a ghostly clown of circuses past to hang out.

The motel was featured in a 2015 episode of Zak Bagans's *Ghost Adventures* and has appeared in countless movies. But let's not forget that the Clown Motel sits next door to, and in full view of, the old Tonopah Cemetery. Walk right out the front door, and there's the cemetery. So, if there aren't enough ghosts to suit you at the motel, you'll surely find a few here. And stepping back into the motel, you may begin to wonder, which is worse, clowns or ghosts? You'll have to decide that on your own.

Ghosts of the Old Tonopah Cemetery

*T*he old Tonopah Cemetery faces the Clown Motel. According to feng shui, that's not a good thing. But it works well for the ghosts who are said to wander over to the motel when the mood strikes. Established in 1901, the cemetery was only used for ten years. After many graves were destroyed by tailings from the Tonopah Extension Mill washing over them, a new location northward was found for the town cemetery.

The most famous resident here at these dusty old grounds that make up the old Tonopah Cemetery is Big Bill Murphy, the hero of the tragic Belmont fire on February 23, 1911. Before he succumbed to his own death, Murphy managed to save several of his fellow miners who were trying to escape the deadly flames. Without a thought of danger, Big Bill jumped into a mine cage and went down to the 1,100-foot level to rescue as many men as he could.

As he descended for his third rescue mission, Bill called out, "Well, boys, I have made two trips and I am nearly all in, but I will try again."

Sadly, he perished during his last trip. But Big Bill Murphy is not forgotten here in Tonopah; he is a hero, and a statue honoring him stands in front of the post office.

Among the other permanent residents here at the old cemetery is Sheriff Tom Logan, who was killed in 1907 at the Jewel, the local brothel, while visiting his girlfriend, May Biggs, Jewel proprietress, in the nearby town of Manhattan.

Victims of the deadly 1905 Tonopah plague as well as those of the 1911 Belmont mine fire disaster rest here.

Perhaps one of them is the ghostly man I saw on the night I visited the cemetery with Zak Bagans and a group of friends. Long past midnight, this was an impromptu visit. Everyone seemed to go in different directions, lost in their own thoughts. I was talking with those who resided there, not sure if they could hear me or not, but assuring them that this was a friendly and oh-so-temporary stop. A tall, shadowy figure approached. I assumed it was Zak. He stood a few feet from me. "This is such a lonely place," I said, kicking sand in emphasis.

He didn't answer. "It's so forlorn. I wonder if there really are any ghosts here," I said. "What do you think?"

No answer. I turned around to see if he was listening—and no one was standing near me. It happens. And you get used to it. Nonetheless, I shivered at the thought that I might have been speaking to the ghost of long-dead Big Bill Murphy, or to one of the men who perished in that long-ago disaster at the mine.

Devil in Tonopah

Known as "Devil" because of the jokes and pranks he liked playing on people, George Davis was Tonopah's first African American resident and businessmen. He is another of those ghosts who likes to mix it up by haunting more than one location. The ghostly Davis spends his time haunting the old Tonopah Cemetery as well as the Tonopah Liquor Company where he worked.

Together with his wife Ruth, Davis bought the Eureka Saloon, which was a popular establishment with Tonopah's African American residents. Though well liked as the leader of the African American community, George Davis was an abusive husband to his wife, who silently bore his cruelty. He shot at her, beat her with anything he could get his hands on, and forced her to work as a prostitute. When she didn't make enough money in Tonopah to suit him, he forced her to travel to Bodie, California, where she worked in the brothels.

In a time when women, especially women of color, had little recourse, Ruth Davis finally decided to leave her husband after he'd beaten her terribly. She'd had enough of his cruelty and cheating with other women. On Saturday, June 21, 1907, she spent the day drinking whiskey and absinthe and smoking opium, a deadly combination. Intoxicated to the point of madness, her anger was fierce. Devil Davis was kind to everyone but her. And this thought only intensified her rage toward him. She would leave, but first she would rest. She awoke early in the morning on June 22 and started to pack. While going through a drawer, she found the gun her husband called Whistling Pete. A smile crossed her face as she picked up the gun. She knew what she must do.

There was no need to speak. Whistling Pete was about to speak for her. Holding the gun, she walked into the Eureka where she found Davis standing at the craps table with friends. She walked up behind him, took aim, and fired four shots into the unsuspecting Davis's back. Gunfire was the last sound George "Devil" Davis heard.

While visiting the old cemetery late one night, a friend recorded EVP that was nothing but the sound of gunfire. Was the ghostly Davis remembering those last moments of his life? We concluded that he was indeed remembering and that this EVP was the sound of the pistol he called Whistling Pete.

Ruth Davis's trouble did not end with the death of Devil Davis. She was arrested and convicted of manslaughter because of her late husband's abuse. She was sentenced to one year at the state prison in Carson City. And during her time there, 1907–1908, Ruth was the only woman at the facility.

An article in the *Tonopah Daily Bonanza* on September 25, 1907, ends with a very telling sentence: "She is the only female occupant of the prison, and it is possible that she will be assigned to the kitchen, as she is said to be a good cook."

Bina Verrault

*N*evada's history is filled with tragic tales of mining and miners, and of the women who came to the mining towns seeking their fortunes in ways that weren't always legal and often relegated them to the lowest rungs of society. Bina Verrault was one such woman. Born in Ironton, Wisconsin, her childhood had not been easy. Her father died in a drunken barroom brawl, and her mother died after an all-night drunk. Bina Finnegan made her own way. She changed her name to Bina Forrester and was living in a Philadelphia boarding house when she met and married New York artist Robert Verrault. Not satisfied with the money her husband made, Bina devised a scheme to increase her wealth. Writing romantic letters to would-be suitors, Bina bilked them out of all she could.

When they discovered her treachery, many of the men were too embarrassed to go to the police. Those who weren't demanded swift justice.

Bina was running from the law and her shady past when she arrived in Tonopah in 1907. Once the most prominent woman in New York, Bina had formed what was dubbed the Love Syndicate, a scheme in which Bina and other young women bilked wealthy widowers out of their fortunes with wine and Spiritualist messages from the grave. The spirits told gullible men that relatives from beyond were showing them where to invest their money. And when they did, it all went to Bina and her cohorts. When the money ran out, so did the young ladies. When Bina wasn't using séances to induce men to turn over their cash, she was making promises of love and devotion.

When it all came crashing down, the law stepped in and arrested Bina, charging her with three crimes. Somehow she was able to pack up and flee the state. Calling herself Mrs. Hamilton, Bina arrived in Tonopah with a few fine gowns and very little money in her possession. She had found the perfect place to hide out. She still had her charm. And using that charm to her advantage in a town of few women, Bina was able to live a comfortable life. In the end it wasn't the law that caught up with Bina but her alcoholism.

The men of Tonopah whom she'd charmed were soon disgusted with the hateful drunk she had become. She spent the last week of her life struggling in and out of an alcoholic stupor. Within less than a year of her arrival, Bina was found wrapped in her exquisite kimono in her little house on Florence Avenue. She was thirty-four years old. It was only after her death that the truth of the scheming Bina Verrault came out.

The resident ghost at the Tonopah Historic Mining Park is Bina Verrault. The ghostly Bina has been seen and felt in the park's visitor center many times. This is the area of town where she lived, and she probably feels very comfortable here.

Speaking of Ghosts at the Vanwood Variety Store

The Vanwood Variety Store is located in the stone building on the corner of Brougher Avenue and Main Street, across from the Mizpah Hotel. Built by George Golden in 1902 to serve as the Nye County Bank, it was the first permanent stone building in Tonopah. Rumor is that the building is haunted by a former bank employee who died in the basement and has decided to stay on. During a recent visit to Tonopah, I stopped in the store and asked about ghosts. You'd be surprised how many people are kind enough to share their ghost experiences with you. Wanda was no exception.

Wanda's young grandson skips happily through the store as she tells me about the ghosts she has encountered in the area surrounding the store, and there have been many. The ghost she remembered most vividly was a ghostly crying woman, just down the block, that she'd managed to help. She spoke at length, and as she did so I wondered if the ghost might be one of the women who worked in Tonopah's early red-light district. After all, it was only a few blocks from the building.

I asked Wanda what she thought, and she agreed it was possible. Then she assured me that all the ghosts here in the store are friendly. She knows this because whenever she is alone in the store and happens to hear them, the ghostly disembodied voices are laughing and chatting. Not once has she ever been frightened. She realizes that these ghosts don't mean anyone any harm.

Ghosts in a Ghost Town: Belmont

Belmont is yet another of Nevada's ghost towns. An 1865 silver discovery led to the establishment of Belmont; two years later, the town had grown significantly, and it was selected to be the county seat for Nye County. In 1875, construction of the courthouse began. Belmont would soon be able to take care of the county's business. By the summer of 1876, work on the new courthouse was completed, and it was ready to serve Nye County in its official capacity.

Although the building still stands to this day, it has long since been abandoned as the county courthouse. With the turn of the twentieth century, silver was discovered at Tonopah. People left Belmont for that city, hoping to strike it rich there. As Tonopah's population increased, that of Belmont fell sharply. And Belmont lost its county seat status to Tonopah.

Many who've visited the old courthouse believe it is haunted. Empaths, those who can sense such things, know it is. They tell of feelings of hopelessness and sadness in the old building. The ghosts who haunt the old Belmont Courthouse are most likely those of Jack Walker and Charlie McIntyre, two men who were lynched at the jail near the site of the building on June 4, 1874. According to one story, the groaning ghostly figures most often appear on full moon nights during the summer months. There are several different accounts of the gruesome lynching; supposedly the walls of the jail were splattered with the blood of the two men, who were beaten nearly to death before being hanged. Angry at the injustice being done to him, one of the men placed a curse on the town of Belmont in his dying breath.

If that is true, his ghost would be happy to know that Belmont is a shadow of its former self, having lost its county seat status thirty years after his murder.

Pioche Ghosts

*N*evada's ghost towns are all that remain of men and women's high hopes of striking it rich in the latest silver discovery. Pioche is such a town. Located approximately 175 miles northeast of Las Vegas, Pioche is like many of Nevada's other ghost towns; it's not been completely abandoned. And just about a thousand people, give or take, make their home here in Pioche.

There are a few businesses that cater to the tourists who come to see Pioche's million-dollar courthouse and Boot Hill Cemetery—how it once was. The cost to build the Lincoln County Courthouse wasn't actually a million dollars; it was only $75,000. But considering that this was in 1872, that was a lot of money. And did I mention that it only took Lincoln County fifty-eight years to pay off the debt incurred in building their courthouse?

Those wanting to stay for the night are welcomed at the Overland Hotel & Saloon, where Zak Bagans and *Ghost Adventures* investigated several years ago. Rumor among ghost-hunting types has it that one or two of the rooms here at the Overland Hotel are haunted. Employees and patrons have had countless encounters with a ghostly woman. No one is quite sure just who she might have been.

Eastern Nevada

The Truth Will Out, Thanks to a Ghost

Carlin is a small town that was created by the Central Pacific Railroad Company in 1868 with the construction of the transcontinental railroad. Named by the railroad in honor of Civil War brigadier general William Passmore Carlin, the new town grew and prospered for the next twenty years, with a rail yard and a roundhouse built by the railroad. Something I find exciting is that recent research by the Carlin Historical Society has revealed that Carlin may have had the first public library in the state of Nevada. As a reader and a writer, I'd say that is definitely something to boast about.

Ghost enthusiasts will be interested in a different aspect of Carlin's history that took place in 1889—a murder that was uncovered thanks to a ghost.

Our tale begins in the fall of 1888 when Mr. and Mrs. George Brewer moved to Carlin and rented a little four-room house, complete with cellar. As a correspondent for the *Elko Free Press*, Mrs. Brewer informed readers of her Busy Bee column about her new home, boasting, "It is a little exciting when one has the good luck to move into a veritable haunted house. . . . So far the ghost hasn't scared us but he is here just the same."

The fun soon turned to annoyance, with the ghost keeping the Brewers awake by tapping on their headboard and rambling loudly through the kitchen. But most of the ghostly activity was in the cellar. And one night Mr. Brewer had had enough. Assuming that the noises were most likely stray cats, he went down into the cellar to see what was going on. There were no cats. And nothing was amiss.

Curious, he began poking at the earthen cellar floor with a shovel. It wasn't long before the shovel struck something hard—like bone. Mr. Brewer began digging intently. When he uncovered a human skull and dismembered sections of a human body, Mr. Brewer put down his shovel and raced upstairs. He would notify the sheriff.

The charred body was dug up and the clothes examined for identification. None was found, but luckily someone recognized a knife in the victim's pocket. That knife had belonged to Miles Faucett. Miles Faucett had last been seen in the company of Josiah and Elizabeth Potts. And coincidentally, the Pottses were the previous tenants of the house Mr. and Mrs. Brewer were living in. Clearly the Pottses had some explaining to do.

Once the body was removed from the cellar, the ghostly activity stopped. Miles Faucett had been found, and the law was on the trail of his killers. Mr. Faucett could now rest in peace.

Josiah and Elizabeth Potts were the most notorious to face trial in the old Elko Courthouse. On March 14, 1889, they were found guilty of murdering and mutilating Miles Faucett and were sentenced to death for their crime. On June 30, 1889, in the early morning before the summer heat overtook Elko, the Pottses were brought to the gallows that had been erected in the courtyard behind the courthouse.

After a brief exchange with her husband, Elizabeth looked toward the sky and said, "God help me, I am innocent."

Josiah added, "God knows we are innocent," as the black hoods were slipped over their heads. The condemned were hanged, one after the other. Josiah was first to go. According to witnesses, Elizabeth Potts's execution was unsightly. The corpulent Elizabeth, dressed in a creamy white frock, stood silently as the noose was slipped around her neck. The stays were cut, but the rope couldn't support her weight, and her neck was nearly severed. Witnesses turned away in horror as blood gushed from her carotid artery, covering her white dress. Elizabeth Potts is the first and only woman to be executed by the state of Nevada.

Twenty years after the Pottses' execution, county commissioners made a decision: it was time Elko County had a larger, more prestigious courthouse. In 1910, the old brick building where the Pottses had stood trial was demolished, and a neoclassical-style courthouse was erected, at a cost of $150,000, at the same location on the corner of Sixth and Idaho Streets.

While Josiah seems to have moved on, Elizabeth Potts has not. According to some courthouse employees, the ghostly Elizabeth roams the courthouse halls and the parking lot, still wearing her blood-soaked execution dress.

Ghosts of the Old Overland Hotel

*W*hen I spoke with Ella B. Trujillo of the Carlin Historical Society about Carlin's history and of the ghost walk she was planning, she said, "There are some stories about the old Overland Hotel." She laughed and added, "Every town probably had an Overland Hotel."

She's right, they did—and some of them had ghost stories attached. The Overland Hotel in Carlin was the site of two killings at the Chinese restaurant located in the hotel.

It was around five o'clock on the morning of January 6, 1924. The temperature sat at about twelve degrees below zero, snow covered the sidewalks, and it was a month before Nevada used lethal gas for the first time as a means of execution. Harry Hunter walked into the café and called for a waiter. Charlie Gee stepped from the kitchen with a smile on his face. Hunter pulled his gun and fired at Gee, who fell to the floor mortally wounded.

Hunter didn't try to run. He was still there holding the gun when Constable Berning arrived moments later. In his dying breath, Charlie Gee called for justice against his killer. Ghost researchers know that a victim's anger and shock at their sudden death can give rise to a ghost. It's possible that the fleeting shadow that is sometimes seen is none other than the ghostly Charlie Gee who still wanders the area of the old Overland Hotel.

Years later, a particularly gruesome murder occurred at the old Overland. The owner/cook at the Chinese restaurant in the hotel had a son who was confined to the state mental hospital in Sparks. Occasionally the young man was permitted to visit his father in Carlin.

The day of the murder, the son was helping chop vegetables in the kitchen while his father waited tables. Suddenly the son stopped working and calmly walked into the dining room wielding the knife.

Without a word, he struck his father with the knife and began cutting the unfortunate man's head off.

This story is well known in Carlin, although it isn't so easily found in newspaper files. It also accounts for any sightings of a headless ghost who walks the area in front of where the old Overland Hotel once stood.

Patsy's Not Leaving

*E*illey Bowers, one of the first Comstock millionaires and famous Washoe seeress, was forced to move from her beloved Bowers Mansion after the death of her husband, Sandy. But Eilley hasn't left the property. She loved her home so much that she has returned to spend eternity there. Singer Frank Sinatra was forced out of his Cal Neva Lodge for hosting a known Mafia member, Sam Giancana. Like Eilley, Sinatra has returned to his old stomping grounds at Tahoe and is happily haunting the place. All this proves is that a ghost who loved a place in life may return to the location and stay forever. Such is the case of Patsy Patterson.

Patsy Patterson coveted the Overland Hotel in downtown Carlin and desperately wanted to lease the place. For whatever reason, there was a snafu, and the owners and their agents refused to acknowledge Patsy or his offer. Desperate to make his point of how unfairly they'd treated him, Patsy went to the hot springs in Elko in the dead of winter. He rented a room and went to the swimming pool. Yes, they would see how terribly they'd treated Patsy. He dove off the ladder headfirst, breaking his neck.

Patsy dutifully left two letters behind. The first was to the Elko newspaper. It read as follows:

> Elko, December 1910
> Just a line to say that I am going to a watery grave on account of Mr. Williams of the First National Bank of Elko. Mr. Williams and Mr. J. Isola of Carlin have not done wrong with me. But all my friends goodbye. God bless you all. Patsy Patterson

The second letter was to his wife, and in it he implored her never to remarry.

And now we'll head back to Carlin, where the Overland Hotel once stood. Here I'll remind you of Eilley Bowers and Frank Sinatra as we ponder whether the ghostly Patsy Patterson was responsible for any of the strange activity that took place at the old hotel.

A Ghost's Gotta Do What a Ghost's Gotta Do

*A*nother ghost who is likely to wander a certain area of a Carlin sidewalk is that of Simon Barclay, who didn't receive justice for his murder at the hands of William Garrard.

On a warm October day in 1879, William Garrard encountered Simon Barclay in front of Jones's store in Carlin. Garrard pulled his gun, pushed it against Barclay's ribcage, and pulled the trigger. As people gathered around the fatally injured Barclay, he dropped to the sidewalk crying, "I've been shot. I am to die."

Garrard was taken into custody, and a trial date was set in Elko, twenty-three miles distant. Apparently judges and juries in the nineteenth century had strange ideas about what constitutes justice. When the facts came out, they told an age-old tale: Mrs. Garrard and Simon Barclay had been involved in an extramarital romance. William Garrard thought about it. There was no other choice. Barclay had to die. And so he armed himself and waited until his next encounter with his wife's lover.

According to the judge and jury, Garrard was justified. He happily walked out of jail a free man, and we can only imagine what went on at the Garrard house next. As for Simon Barclay, he is no doubt a ghost seeking justice for his untimely death. If you should come upon him some dark night in Carlin, step aside. He has no idea that a century has come and gone since that long-ago October day.

The Cook Refused to Leave the Train

*N*evada has a rich railway history that includes the Chinese immigrants who provided the labor that built the railroads that crisscrossed the state. There are a few stories of ghostly railcars in Nevada's lore. The story of the ghostly cook has been told and retold for years.

One winter night in 1889, a Chinese cook working on the railroad near Elko got into a heated argument with another man over his cooking abilities. Apparently the other man was unhappy with the meals the cook had been providing. The cook was offended; he considered himself a good cook and didn't take the insults lightly. As they raised their voices, the men began shoving each other. And then they began throwing punches. The unfortunate cook was beaten to death in the fight. This is not the end of our story.

The ghostly cook decided to stay on and jealously guard his kitchen. But the trouble really started when he began appearing to workers in the kitchen. The encounters were not always friendly, as the cook wasn't pleased with the way the new people were rearranging the utensils and tools. When he appeared to them holding a butcher knife, the kitchen crew walked out and refused to work in the haunted railcar. People came and went, but no one stayed once they'd encountered the angry cook. The railroad company decided to retire the haunted car.

Haunted Express Car No. 5

January 1882 and Wells Fargo and Company's Express Car No. 5 on the Central Pacific had a problem—a problem of a ghostly nature. And every passenger on the train that ran from San Francisco, California, to Ogden, Utah, had experienced similar ghostly problems. They blamed the ghost on the accidental death of a conductor on the train as it made its way past Truckee, California. No one wanted to work on Express Car No. 5.

Those unlucky enough to have to work on it knew that they would hear strange noises on the roof of the car and see items tossed about as the train rolled across the landscape. One passenger was so frightened that he waited until the train slowed and then jumped off somewhere near Wadsworth. Later he would say that there had been a coffin on board, and the coffin's occupant had sat up, looked around, and happily called the messenger by name before vanishing. No wonder he jumped off the train.

Everyone was well aware of the ghostly goings-on on Express Car No. 5, but when men began refusing to work in the car, the company was faced with a decision.

Ghost in a Cave

*O*n July 7, 1887, J. T. Baker's letter to the editor appeared in the *Eureka Daily Sentinel.* In the letter, Baker told of coming face-to-face with the ghost of a soldier in a cave in the Ruby Valley. Of that encounter, he wrote:

> I wish to state at the onset that my observation of, and conversation with, this mysterious being, call him ghost, spirit or mortal man, as you please, have changed my belief in things spiritual or supernatural, which belief I considered as firm as the rock of Gibraltar. As far back as I remember, I have always treated with ridicule and derision any suggestion of things supernatural, but I had first by a somewhat frightful and later more pleasant experience, that I was wrong in my dogmatic ideas and that spirits do exist.
>
> In my second interview the soldier told me that although he had all the appearance of a material being, that in fact it was only in form and appearance; that there was no tangible substance composing his form as it appeared. This I demonstrated to be true to my entire satisfaction by placing my hand on his arm as I supposed, but my hand met no resisting substance, any more than passing your hand through a sunbeam, passing through an orifice in a darkened room.
>
> He went on to say that he had the power of speech which is something very rare among the spirits; that some communicate to people on earth by means of raps, some by writing; and in various ways; that he did have the power to speak but did not know how long it would continue. . . . He stated that he'd enlisted in the

regular army in 1881 at Fort Leavenworth, Kansas and supposed that he would be sent south, but he was not.

The ghostly soldier went on to tell Baker that he had fallen in love with the beautiful daughter of a Ruby Valley rancher, and luckily her parents had approved of him. Unfortunately, the post commander was also smitten with the young lady and refused to grant the soldier any more time off.

When she was told that the soldier was missing and presumed dead, the young lady was overcome with grief, as were her parents. They sold the ranch and moved eastward, leaving the solider to give up on life. The ghost ended his tale by explaining that he'd come to the cave and had taken his own life. As punishment for this reckless act, he was forever doomed to spend eternity there in the lonely cave.

Although he swore it was true, many people in Eureka doubted the veracity of Baker's story. If you should go spelunking in a cave in the Ruby Valley, you might just encounter the ghostly soldier—or not.

Hank Parish

*H*ank Parish swung into eternity for the murder of P. G. Thompson. . . . The trap was now sprung and the resulting fall instantly broke the wretch's neck." Thus the *Ely Record* of December 20, 1890, reported on the execution of Hank Parish, the first man legally hanged in Ely.

Parish had asked for a change of venue from Lincoln County to White Pine County, arguing that people in Lincoln County were prejudiced against him. And on October 13, 1890, he went on trial for the cold-blooded knife murder of P. G. Thompson during a card game in Royal City on the night of August 3, 1890.

Hank Parish was a thoroughly bad hombre with a terrible reputation. It was believed that he had killed at least eighteen men. The jury had no trouble in seeing the truth. The deliberations lasted an hour. And at the end of the three-day trial, Parish was found guilty of murder in the first degree and sentenced to death. It was reported that he spent his last night on earth laughing and joking with jailers until long after midnight.

After the execution was carried out, Parish's body was left on display in the courthouse for a few hours, then taken out to the cemetery and buried in an unmarked grave. The bad man may have been forgotten, but he wasn't gone.

Strange things have been happening here since the hanging of Hank Parish. Among the ghostly occurrences reported in the courthouse and annex building are unexplained cold drafts, deep disembodied laughter, heavy footsteps, and creaking stairs. All seem to indicate that a ghostly presence is in residence. There may be some doubt as to the ghost's identity, but I believe that, yes, the shadowy figure that paranormal investigators have spotted near the elevators is indeed the ghostly Hank Parish.

Christmas at Treasure Hill

Myrrh is mine; its bitter perfume
Breathes a life of gathering gloom;
Sorrowing, sighing,
Bleeding, dying,
Sealed in the stone-cold tomb.
                              —John Henry Hopkins Jr.,
                              "We Three Kings of Orient Are"

*Q*uick! Think of a holiday associated with ghosts. I bet you thought of Halloween. What about Christmas? Sure, there is the mistletoe, the wreaths, the shiny ornaments, and the Christmas tree. But during the Victorian era, sharing ghost stories at Christmastime was a popular endeavor. And let's not forget that Charles Dickens's classic 1843 tale, *A Christmas Carol*, is a ghost story. Delighting ghost hunters, and those who write about ghosts, is the fact that Edward Pola and George Wyle's ever-popular Christmas song "It's the Most Wonderful Time of the Year" mentions ghost stories.

In researching the paranormal, you will find many cases of apparitions that appear only once a year—anniversary ghosts, if you will. And they usually appear during an anniversary or a holiday that was meaningful to them. At Treasure Hill, there were the ghosts who came together at Christmas to share and enjoy a big feast.

In 1868, a discovery of silver ore led to a boom at Treasure Hill. The boom was short-lived and over within two years. In those two years, murders and mayhem were commonplace. The most horrendous was in all likelihood the murder of one mining partner by the other. After killing his victim, the murderer calmly took an axe and chopped off the victim's head and feet.

The killer managed to escape the long arm of the law. His victim may well have been one of the ghosts who appeared at Treasure Hill on Christmas 1878.

There were not many people here anymore. The silver, along with the opportunities it represented, had long since given out. On a snowy Christmas night on Treasure Hill, at a long-abandoned house, a group of ghosts gathered to partake of a phantoms' feast. The table was covered with the finest of damask cloth. Two large candelabras cast an eerie light as ghostly waiters served the finest of meals on gleaming silver platters.

After their feast, the ghosts were said to have enjoyed wine and whiskey. In their revelry, they laughed and sang loudly until the clock struck midnight, signaling the end of Christmas and the arrival of a new day. All was silent and dark in the old house once again.

The Hamilton Mystery

*H*amilton, at the base of Treasure Hill, is another of Nevada's boom-and-bust mining towns that became ghost towns when the silver played out. Located about fifty miles west of Ely, Hamilton boasted over twelve thousand residents in 1869. Serving them were dozens of saloons, stores, dance halls, theaters, and every other business that made life in the Nevada desert bearable. It didn't last. Within a few short years, Hamilton was little more than a ghost town.

Our story was recounted by a longtime Nevada resident, Mrs. Eva May Gill. In 1871, she and her parents were living in Eastern California in the Owens River Valley where she met her future husband, William James Gill. The couple was married in 1872 and moved to Hamilton.

After she saw an article in the *Reno Gazette* that told of bleached bones, a rusty knife, and a rifle being found at the bottom of a mineshaft near Hamilton, Mrs. Gill decided to share her husband's ghostly tale. The details of her letter appeared in the October 31, 1929, issue of the *Reno Gazette*.

> One night in the early 1860s William Gill was traveling on the trail between Hamilton and Treasure Hill when he was suddenly overcome with feelings of anxiety—something in the darkness was dreadfully wrong. Gill was alone on the trail that he knew well. Still, he could sense there was something out here on this night that he wasn't meant to encounter. As the hair on the back of his neck rose up, he knew he would not go any further on this night. He slowed his horse, yanked the reins, and turned around.
>
> A few evenings later my husband was sitting in a crowded saloon when a man came rushing in and

reported he had seen a ghost on the trail. His description was so vivid that the crowd became interested and started out to find the ghost, boastfully saying that no ghost could scare them.

When they approached the spot they saw a tall object with long white hair and beard, robed in white, pacing back and forth across the trail between a cottonwood tree and a clump of willows, looking neither to the right or left.

The entire crowd, so the story goes, halted and not one had the courage to approach the white robed, bewhiskered figure.

The Hamilton ghost story was related time and again in the early days of that camp and was one of the mysteries that were never explained.

Justice at Hamilton

*E*dward Crutchley shot and killed John Howlett one spring day in 1886 for stealing two of his horses. Crutchley didn't deny the murder. How could he with so many witnesses? After a swift trial, the jurors deliberated a short time before finding Crutchley guilty and sentencing him to death.

On December 31, 1886, he was hanged from the Withington Building, and after being laid out for public viewing, Crutchley was buried at Hamilton Cemetery, aka Mourner's Point Cemetery. For many years afterward, it was said that Crutchley's moans and cries for mercy could be heard on certain nights in the old cemetery.

Ghosts at the Old Lander County Courthouse in Austin

*A*ustin is a tiny town in the middle of Nevada on the western slopes of the Toiyabe Range. With fewer than two hundred residents today, it's hard to believe that there were nearly ten thousand people living here in Austin at one time. Like other Nevada mining towns, it was the 1862 silver discovery that brought people here. Within a few years, Austin was the second-largest city in Nevada and was designated the county seat of Lander County.

On October 30, 1868, twenty-one-year-old Rufus B. Anderson was hanged in Austin for killing Noble T. Slocum, who refused to pay Rufus's mother the money he owed her. The execution of Anderson is noteworthy in that it took three attempts to successfully hang the heavyset man.

The Lander County Courthouse was built in 1871. And it's believed that both Rufus B. Anderson and Richard Jennings haunt the building. Jennings was among the thousands who came to Austin hoping to strike it rich. Instead he lost his temper and sealed his fate when he shot and killed John A. Barrett, a popular Austin rancher, after a brief argument at the International Hotel. While awaiting trial, Jennings was taken out of jail and lynched at the courthouse on December 14, 1881, for the senseless murder.

The December 13–14, 1881, issue of the *Daily Reese River Reveille* reported on Barrett's murder and the subsequent lynching of Jennings:

> We are again called on to record another fatal shot from which John A. Barrett, an old and much respected citizen of Austin, was almost instantly killed. Somewhere between 10 and 11 o'clock last night, Barrett was in the barroom of the International Hotel when a man

by the name of Richard Jennings sought trouble with him when some angry words passed. The matter was shortly quieted down and quickly settled. In the course of 15 minutes afterwards, Barrett asked Jennings in a friendly manner to take a drink at the bar. Immediately following which, and while standing up against the counter, Barrett turned from Jennings to engage in conversation with another person when Jennings drew a Smith and Wesson's self-cocking revolver and fired three shots and either from the first or the second shot the ball entered Barrett's back, immediately under the right shoulder blade, striking the spinal cord. When the wounded man turned around, apparently paralyzed, being unable to speak, he fell to the floor on his face, dying almost immediately.

Between 1 and 2 this morning Richard Jennings, who shot and killed John A. Barrett the night before, was hung in front of the courthouse building. As near as we have been able to gather the facts connected with the hanging of Jennings they are as follows:

About half past one o'clock this morning a party of masked men numbering about 25 persons, well-armed, went to the courthouse and with a sledgehammer broke down a door from the main hall into a room between the sheriff's front office and the jail and on entering a gun or guns were levelled in close proximity to James Parrish's head, deputy sheriff who was lying in bed and who was held in abeyance. The key to the jail was then taken out of the Deputy Sheriff's pocket, and after an unsuccessful search for the key to the cell in which Jennings was confined, a sledgehammer was used, apparently one blow, when the key was found and the cell door opened and Jennings taken therefrom.

He was brought through the Deputy Sheriff's room with a rawhide lariat around his neck, and as he passed by the Sheriff's bed he cast a wistful look in that direction, evidently wanting to say something, but doubtless afraid to open his mouth, as he saw the inevitable crisis at hand. He was led to the front door by the leather necktie, and placed on the platform outside the main front entrance to the courthouse building, and the other end of the lariat was thrown up to the portice of the second story—

Before he was drawn up, Jennings was heard to say, "Oh my God. Boys, I guess I deserve this."

So far as known to us, the act is endorsed by all. While of course, all good citizens oppose resorting to unlawful means in the punishment of criminals, yet for the protection of life and property, it sometimes becomes absolutely necessary to resort to Judge Lynch.

Both Anderson's and Jennings's ghosts are thought to be in residence at the former Lander County Courthouse. They are responsible for the sound of occasional loud sobbing that is heard in the building, as well as the creaking and heavy footsteps on the stairs. They have been known to irritate those who work here by moving items from one spot to another.

On the anniversary of his lynching, Jennings's ghost is reportedly seen in the old jail from where he was pulled to his cruel fate.

The Old Austin Elementary School

*Y*ou can't talk about ghosts in Austin without hearing about the ghost at the old Austin Elementary School on Sixth Street. Built in 1926, the building has also been known as the Lander County High School, the Austin High School, and most recently the Austin Elementary School. Listed on the National Register of Historic Places, the old school is, at this writing, up for sale.

According to local lore, a long-ago principal of the school was so despondent that he hanged himself at the school one night. Ever since that time, strange things have happened in the building. A shadowy figure has been seen pacing near the front door of the school at dusk. And those who've worked alone in the building after dark tell of hearing loud moaning and sobbing that seems to move in different areas of the building.

The Ghost Lady of Austin

In a time before twenty-four-hour news, the internet, and phones with cameras, it was easy to get lost in the crowd. So there is no record of who she might have been. Nor is there any information on who she may have been looking for. Your guess is as good as the next on where Austin's ghost lady might be haunting tonight.

The beautiful ghost first appeared suddenly at dusk in a private home in the summer of 1879. Those who saw her said she was clad in a long white dress, and a whooshing sound followed her as she made her way through the house and out into the garden. While the startled homeowners watched, she went several yards from the garden and vanished into thin air.

Perhaps she was trying to relay a message or a warning. She may even have had a familial connection to someone who was at the home that long-ago evening. Worse, someone there may have been responsible for the lady being a ghost in the first place. Whoever she was, the ghost lady of Austin is likely just another mystery that will never be solved.

A Ghost in Paradise Valley

*P*aradise Valley is a ghost town located forty miles north of Winnemucca (one of the places Johnny Cash and Willie Nelson boasted about being in the song "I've Been Everywhere"). A farming community with little more than a hundred residents, Paradise Valley's claim to fame is actress Edna Purviance, who was born here in 1895. When she was a teenager, the family relocated to Lovelock. As a teenager, Edna dreamed of a life of glamour and wealth. In hopes of fulfilling her dreams, she ran away to San Francisco where she met the dashing Charlie Chaplin, and the rest is silent-screen history.

No, Edna is not our ghost. That honor goes to an elderly man by the name of Furman. In 1875, several years after he died, Mr. Furman came back and began haunting an area outside the Silver State Flour Mill. There the ghostly old man would appear before teenage boys and kindly dispense sage advice to them. The old building was listed on the National Register of Historic Places in 1976 and is still standing. The teenage boys have grown up and have long gone to their own graves; there's no word on whether or not the ghostly old Mr. Furman is still hanging around offering wisdom and advice.

Ghostly Conductor

Like the ghostly hitchhiker who appears in ghost stories across the United States, variations of a ghostly conductor are told in many locations. The ghostly conductor of Nevada ghost lore is located somewhere near Carlin. For the last several decades, passengers and crew have spotted him just up ahead on the tracks, swinging his lantern in warning. There is no danger, and the train moves on by without incident. But this ghost story may be the outcome of an actual event.

On the evening of August 12, 1939, the luxurious Streamliner City of San Francisco pulled out of Carlin heading west. The train was running at least thirty minutes late and would have to pick up speed in order to make it to Oakland on time. The engineer increased the train's speed to ninety miles an hour. Fifteen miles out of Carlin, disaster struck when the train derailed in a horrendous crash in Palisade Canyon. Five of the train's fifteen cars were completely demolished, and a bridge spanning the Humboldt River was destroyed. Twenty-four people, including passengers and crew, were killed in the accident; more than a hundred people were seriously injured.

After lengthy investigations, it was determined that the derailment was the result of saboteurs. But who would do such a thing, and why would they do it? Answers to those questions were never discovered.

The ghostly conductor has been seen in the pouring rain and in a raging snowstorm. Perhaps he is someone who lost his life that night in 1939 and hopes to prevent another such disaster.

Eureka

*N*evadans are a friendly lot. None more so than in the tiny town of Eureka, one of Nevada's friendliest towns. According to local legend, Eureka received its name when a miner discovered silver and yelled out, "Eureka!"

The town was settled in 1864 when silver was discovered nearby. A mining district was created that same year, and as Eureka's population increased, it became the county seat of Eureka County in 1873.

History buffs and ghost enthusiasts are happy to know that in addition to being rich in history, Eureka has its fair share of ghosts and hauntings. Zak Bagans and the *Ghost Adventures* team discovered this when they did an episode here for their hit TV show. This little town happily flaunts both its history and its ghosts. Eureka's annual Great Eureka Ghost Hunt is the city's ghost-hunting event and draws people from across the country. Naturally the event takes place during the Halloween season in late October. Heading up the event is Dana Freund, tourism director, ghost tour guide, and owner of Miss Dana's Visit Eureka Nevada Shoppe.

I am proud to have been the special guest for the premier event. During that event, Dana led us on her amazing ghost walk. I don't use the word "amazing" lightly. Dana knows her stuff—the history, the legends, and the ghosts. And she presents it all in a fun-filled hour-and-a-half tour.

One of our first stops was the Jackson House, arguably the most haunted spot in Eureka.

I don't know about that, but I do know the place has its ghosts. You can feel them all around you when you enter the stately old hotel. Built in 1877, the Jackson House was advertised as the only fireproof hotel in Eastern Nevada. True enough, the hotel and a saloon next door withstood Eureka's devastating fire of 1879.

Ghostly children are said to run up and down the stairs. You'll know you've encountered one of the kids when you feel a cold chill on the staircase. I met the ghostly Tony in a kitchen area—a middle-aged man, busy at work, with rolled-up sleeves and a harried look on his face. I tried to persuade him to let go of the work. He wouldn't. "No one works as hard as me," he said.

A former owner of the hotel is said to wander the halls late at night, making sure all is well. Numerous visitors to the Jackson House have seen her as she goes about her nightly chores.

Other ghosts included the grumpy man and the angry woman who stay in the Jackson Suite. Are they from different time periods? Were they a married couple? No one knows for sure, only that they are not very happy.

Traveling can be hard on hairstyles. If you find yours needs some TLC, you'll be happy to know that the haunted Jackson House Hair Salon is located in the Jackson House, and they can do wonders. The ghosts in the salon are the sort that enjoy being part of it all and rarely make themselves known. But if you should catch a glimpse of a woman out of the corner of your eye—you've seen one of them.

I've visited many old jails across Nevada, and I can tell you that there's just something about the ambience within them. If you have claustrophobia, I'd advise you not to go into these cramped old jail cells with heavy crosshatch doors and little light. Okay, you've been warned. Now, come with me and step into an antique jail cell. Do you feel anything? Even those who aren't sensitive can almost feel the anguish of those who've spent time here.

During the tour, Dana asked me to go into the old Eureka jail cell and see what I felt. It wasn't pleasant. As I stood in one of the cells, I felt that someone had suffered pain and was hurting there. I told the group what I felt and quickly stepped out. Paranormal investigator Christopher Counsel asked his K-2 if someone was hurt there, and all lights lit up red—confirmation of sorts, I suppose.

Tunnel Ghosts

*G*host enthusiasts go into some strange places. The tunnels in Eureka are one example. Built by Chinese laborers, the tunnels feature interesting brickwork. Now stop a moment and think about that. These men were down here day and night building these tunnels of brick with barely any ventilation, heat, or light. No wonder there is a heaviness that hangs throughout the tunnels.

Beneath the Afterlife Antiques & Oddities store (located in the old Eureka Cafe), the tunnels have been amazing ghost enthusiasts since Eureka tourism director Dana Freund opened her Miss Dana's Visit Eureka Nevada Shoppe and began her historic walking tours. As a special treat, Dana took me down into the tunnels for a private mini investigation. We collected much photographic and video evidence and felt that there are several ghosts here in the tunnels.

Dinner and Ghosts at the Urban Cowboy Bar and Grill

*I*f you're like me, you love a good enchilada. In fact, I've rarely met an enchilada I didn't like. So it was that a dinner event was planned at the Urban Cowboy Bar and Grill, where Mexican food is the specialty. My mouth was watering by the time I sat down to my plate of chicken enchiladas con frijoles y arroz. *¡Muy delicioso!* And as we enjoyed the meal, we talked of ghosts. This was a ghost hunt after all. When asked about ghosts here at the Urban Cowboy, owner Maria Urena told of the ghosts here being mistaken for *real* kids.

They are playful little ghosts who are occasionally asked not be so noisy. Maria told of a family member who complained that the kids were being too loud one night after the last customer had gone. The restaurant was closed; they were the only two in the restaurant. She calmly told him that the kids were home.

He looked at her and asked, "The ghosts?"

She nodded. The ghosts here are lively but not mischievous or mean. That's something to think about while you sip your mango margarita.

Talking Ghosts and Writing with Trina

*M*iss Dana's Visit Eureka Nevada Shoppe bespeaks an elegance and charm of times past. A place of teapots, teacups, mirrors, and coziness—here Dana Freund teaches manners, the correct way to drink and serve tea, while sharing information about her town of Eureka. While Dana was busy dispensing tea and information to a visiting couple eager to learn more about Eureka, Trina Machacek, author and columnist, and I began a conversation over apple cider tea. As writers, we discussed books and writer's block, which thankfully neither one of us has ever suffered—knock on wood.

But this was a ghost-hunting event during the Halloween season, so naturally the talk turned to ghosts. As we sipped Miss Dana's delicious apple cider tea, Trina told me about the ghost who shares her home located ten miles out of town.

At one time, Trina and her husband owned the local hardware store, which had come with a ghost. Sensing that the ghost was female, and for lack of a better name, they called her Tilly. She never caused any problems, but they realized she was there. When Trina's husband died, she sold the hardware store and began writing full time, both books and her columns that appear in twelve newspapers.

Would Tilly follow her to her house, or would she stay in the building that had housed the hardware store? Trina pondered the question—but she already knew the answer. She could sense Tilly in the house, and that gave her comfort. By using an SLS ghost-hunting app, a visitor to the house confirmed that Tilly was indeed there with Trina. And this makes her happy.

The High School

I'll begin by telling you that half of those I asked about the cemetery under the Eureka County High School assured me that it was nothing but urban legend. Others told me that it was indisputable fact; the high school was built over an early-day cemetery. And we know what that means. Disturbing graves in any fashion can lead to hauntings. One particularly interesting haunting was that of the Black Hope Cemetery in Crosby, Texas. This one was featured on the TV show *Unsolved Mysteries*. Apparently a subdivision of new homes was built over the cemetery—and yes, there were ghostly problems galore. But there are no such problems at the Eureka County High School. I asked. And no one could think of a single ghost story . . . yet.

There is an abandoned Chinese cemetery on Vandal Way across the street from the high school. Only one grave remains here. The rest have been lost or destroyed to time and progress. It is believed that some of the remains of those who rested here were sent back to China for reburial, as was the custom. But there are also those who believe the old cemetery extended much further and that the high school sits atop it.

Bulldog Kate

*N*evada is, for the most part, a live-and-let-live state, with prostitution still legal in many of the state's seventeen counties. Like gambling, mining, and the railroad, prostitution played a role in early-day Nevada's history. And as you might expect, there are a few ghost stories associated with these ladies of the evening.

Those who worked in the profession in the nineteenth century often gave themselves, or were awarded, colorful names. Not all the names were complimentary. As an example, there were Bulldog Kate Miller and Hog Eye Mary Irwin, two women who plied their trade in Eureka 1876. In any profession, there is bound to be some rivalry, but Kate and Mary were more than rivals. They detested each other. Whenever they met, there was bound to be trouble. On the night of September 1, 1876, Kate and Mary were drinking in a saloon on Main Street. The *Eureka Daily Sentinel* on September 5, 1876, reported:

> Kate Miller, better known as "Bulldog Kate" who was stabbed last Friday night in a saloon on N. Main by Mary Irwin alias "Hog Eye Mary," died of her wounds at 3 o'clock and was buried yesterday afternoon.

The article went on to state that Kate was drunk and began loudly insulting Mary, "using the foulest and most abusive language."

Kate Miller was a vicious drunk. She was well known in the police court. She was in and out of jail for her violent behavior. And for some time she'd been making threats against Mary Irwin's life. In an attempt to frighten her, Kate had even broken the door to Mary's little house. Mary was frightened of the woman, who carried a knife and a pistol. But she needed to put a stop to the harassment once and for all. She demanded that Kate meet her outside where they could settle the argument. But as they stepped out of the saloon, Mary pulled a knife and stabbed Kate. Mary was taken to jail and Kate to the morgue. But this wasn't the last of Bulldog Kate.

Two weeks after her untimely death, Kate's disembodied voice was heard in the saloon where she'd met her fate. Not content with staying in the saloon, the ghostly Kate made her way back to her former residence on Buel Street. The *Eureka Daily Sentinel* on September 14, 1876, told the story:

> Haunted—the house on Buel Street formerly occupied by Kate Miller the woman stabbed two weeks ago is haunted. The dis-embodied spirit of the late occupant has returned, and according to the stories told, is moving in a lively manner for one who is supposed to be dead. A woman living next door became so frightened of the racket the ghost was kicking up, that she has vacated the house owned by her, and has gone further down the street. A well-known spiritualist in town intends interviewing the spirit and hold [sic] a séance in the haunted house. If such a meeting takes place there will be a lively time for such parties.
>
> Rest, perturbed spirit, rest.

If you're curious, a jury of twelve men found Mary Irwin not guilty of Kate Miller's murder after her second trial on February 6, 1877.

The Ghost Who Haunted His Killer

*T*he story of Lee Singleton and John Murphy serves as a cautionary tale and is one of Eureka's favorite ghost stories.

John Murphy received no justice in a court of law. His killer, Lee Singleton, covered up his murder so well that no one even realized Murphy was dead. The two men were friends who worked in the mining industry as furnace feeders at the same smelting plant in Eureka. While they worked, Singleton and Murphy often argued with each other. Their arguments weren't heated or bitter, and they didn't last long. After a disagreement, they were soon laughing and talking with each other—until the day that Murphy angrily hit Singleton. That incident changed their friendship.

"I took no notice of it until one day he struck me. He did not know that he signed his death warrant with that blow, but he did," Singleton would later write.

One evening in the middle of their sixteen-hour shift, Murphy stopped working and was nowhere to be found.

Knowing they were friends, a supervisor asked Singleton about Murphy's whereabouts. Singleton shrugged and explained that Murphy had complained about not feeling well, grabbed his coat and hat, and left. The truth was more sinister. If not for Murphy's ghost coming back to haunt him, Lee Singleton might never have confessed. Of the murder, Singleton wrote,

> When the opportunity finally presented itself I stepped behind him and struck him a blow on the head with my shovel as he was stooping to get a scoopful of charcoal. To drag him to the feed hole and throw him on the charge, was but a moment's work. I do not know whether he was dead or only stunned, but it made little difference, as the furnace would have suffocated him

in a moment. By working hard I succeeded in covering the body with ore and charcoal, and as the charge
in the furnace sunk he was soon out of sight, and it
would have been impossible to find the least traces of
him. This work occupied about fifteen minutes.

Filled with remorse at what he'd done, Singleton began seeing
John Murphy's ghostly face staring back at him from the furnace.

It seemed that every shovelful of ore that I flung into
the feed-hole struck on his body and that the bubbling
of the blast took to itself speech and upbraided me
for my cruelty. When burring-out time came I went
to the front of the furnace, it was him that I was stirring up and raking out instead of the clinkers of iron.
My reason told me that the fierce heat had consumed
every portion of him, and that what had not gone off
into the fumes had run out of the front and was now
a component part of the slag-pile; but a hallucination fixed on my brain and I saw him materialized at
every part of the furnace where my work called me. I
got such a mania for looking into the feed-hole of the
furnace that I soon became leaded and incapacitated
from further labor; and on my recovery I could not
procure another situation, as the foreman seemed to
have some suspicion that I was accountable for John's
strange disappearance.

Years passed. Singleton could not stop himself from gazing
into every furnace he came upon in search of John Murphy. Overwhelmed with guilt, he went to his cabin, sat down, and wrote his
confession. When he'd finished his task, Singleton drank a fatal portion of laudanum. His ghost still wanders the area outside Eureka
where his lonely cabin once stood.

The Haunted Cabin on Paul Street

To all outward appearances, Charles Barker had everything going for him. He was well known and well liked in Eureka. Still, he couldn't shake the horrible depression that engulfed him. Hoping to alleviate his pain, Barker sought happiness by moving into the small cabin on Paul Street where two of his friends lived. If anyone could help him out of his despondency, it was his friends. When no one answered his knock at the door, he grabbed the doorknob and turned it.

The door was unlocked, so he walked in, calling to his friends. No one was home. He was alone in the cabin and engulfed in a wave of darkness. Overwhelmed with unbearable sadness, Charles Barker went to the foot of the bed and stood there a moment. There he cut his own throat from ear to ear.

According to an article in the *Eureka Daily Sentinel* on March 28, 1880, Barker's friends were so distraught at his death, they moved out of the cabin—never to return. Then as now, reasonably priced housing was difficult to find. And so it didn't take long before the cabin was once again occupied. Mr. John McRae settled in. This is when the trouble started.

The ghostly Charles Barker returned. And John McRae told anyone who would listen about the ghost who came to the foot of his bed every night, moaning loudly. All agreed it was the ghost of the unfortunate Mr. Barker—but how to rid the cabin of the ghost? No one had the answer to that question. And the ghostly moaning continued night after night—until Mr. John McRae finally decided he'd had enough and moved on. It's doubtful the old cabin is still standing. And what of Charles Barker? Did he move on? Or did he stay at the same location, haunting the next building that was built where the cabin once stood?

A Haunted House in Elko

In the spring of 1918, two men moved into the little house on the hill where an insane woman had recently killed herself. Unfortunately, she didn't go anywhere. And there she stayed, screaming and crying and making the lives of the house's occupants miserable—not to mention that they were losing sleep. Just when the crying stopped, the ghost began knocking on the door and the walls. And according to the *Elko Daily Independent*, April 15, 1918, no one could figure out how to banish the annoying ghost.

Desperate, the owners of the house offered anyone with knowledge of ghosts to come and see what they could do. In exchange, the homeowners would fix the ghost detective up with comfortable dwelling. No one wanted to take on the job.

The homeowners were stubborn and refused to move. And the ghost kept up its antics. Perhaps she is still there somewhere.

Haunted Brothel in Elko

*G*host researchers, ghost investigators, and those who write about ghosts will go anywhere for a ghost and a story. If you don't believe that now, you may change your mind after reading about an experience I had several years ago in Elko.

It was during the Halloween season when ghosts take center stage. I was a guest on a local radio show, taking calls from people who wanted to ask about their ghost. The last caller of the evening claimed to be the owner of a working (legally operated) brothel in Elko. He was being besieged with complaints from the girls about a ghost who was lurking about.

Some may have put the call off as a prank, but this is Nevada and brothels are legal in certain communities. And besides, aren't ghosts everywhere? As he explained the ghost's behavior, I wondered if what was going on at the brothel was place memory or a residual haunting. I asked if anyone ever communicated with the ghost.

"No way!" he replied.

"Is this your only ghost?" I asked.

"Well—the girls seem to think there are others. But he is the scariest."

As we were closing out the call, he suddenly asked, "Would you be willing to come and do a ghost investigation?"

Of course I would. But not so fast—he stayed on the line until after we were off the air. We exchanged contact information with the promise I would think about coming to Elko and looking into his ghost. I'd investigated many old brothels, but a working brothel would be a new experience. Two weeks later, I'd assembled our team, which consisted of Bill and me and EVP specialists Mark and Debby Constantino, and we were on our way.

We interviewed the girls who'd been seeing and experiencing the ghostly man who had the habit of walking in through a side bedroom wall and lingering in the doorway before walking into the closet and vanishing. Others had witnessed the ghosts of two young women in the pole-dance room and the legs of a ghostly woman walking up the stairs. Clearly there was something paranormal going on here.

The pole-dance room had an aura that gave Debby and me the sense that this might be an active area. So we set up our cameras here first. But as so often happens in haunted locations, the cameras stopped working. And all we had to show for our time was nothing but two hours of black screen. The Constantinos were luckier. They managed to capture EVP that said, "Walk with us—we're all alone."

Next we began checking the rooms where the ghostly man appeared. Right away, I could feel that there was some sense of negativity with this ghost. No doubt this was the reason for most of the girls' uneasiness. During the first EVP session with the Constantinos, I looked at the doorway and noticed a dark shadowy figure hovering inches above the floor.

"Why are you here?" I asked.

"Leave me," came the reply.

This particular ghost could not be a place memory. He was interacting.

"We will leave you, if you stop bothering the ladies who live here," Debby said.

Her statement was met with silence.

"What is your name?" I asked.

"Mildred."

There was more research to be done. Hours later, we packed up our equipment and headed back to Reno. We would visit the brothel two more times; in the meantime, I would start researching. When we returned to the brothel, I asked the owner if the building had been altered, as this, we thought, might explain why the ghost came through a side wall.

"They moved the original front door that was where the side door is today," he said.

So, there we had a reason for the ghost's entrance. "There was a robbery here, back in the sixties I believe. The robber thought he had kept all the girls upstairs, but one lady sneaked out and notified the sheriff. He took everyone's money and headed out the front door, but when he got outside, deputies were waiting. There was a shootout, and he was killed."

He frowned. "He's the ghost, isn't he?"

"Most likely," I agreed. "But I think he is nothing more than a residual haunting, imprinted on the environment because of the violent way in which he died."

As far as the ghostly woman's legs, there is a theory among some ghost researchers that ghosts fade away over time. It's possible, I suppose. Still, it doesn't explain the ghost of Anne Boleyn, whose headless ghost has been haunting Blickling Hall and other locations in Great Britain for nearly six centuries. My guess is that the ghostly legs of the brothel are residual.

Ghost on Horseback

Lamoille sits at the base of the Ruby Mountains about nineteen miles southeast of Elko. It is a picturesque little community, first founded 1865. Forty years later, Lamoille's first church, the Little Church of the Crossroads, was built. Lamoille Canyon is known as the Yosemite of Nevada, and like the church, it is a must-see for tourists and photographers.

This tale takes place in the winter of 1892. The people of Lamoille Valley were beset by a ghostly horseman who'd first been seen by George Butler two years earlier. Who was the ghost, and what did he want? No one seemed to know. The rider was described as a cowboy wearing a slouch hat and riding a bald-faced sorrel horse. Neither the horse nor the rider made a sound as they made their way across tall snowdrifts and out into the darkness. Those who were brave enough to go out into the cold night and look for tracks found none.

Even in broad daylight, the ghostly rider and his horse occasionally made an appearance passing close to windows, yet never leaving tracks as evidence of their presence. And that was enough to silence those who said that perhaps there was no ghost at all, only some young man playing a prank.

The Ghost and Hiram Chase

*N*ew Yorker Hiram Chase came to Nevada by way of the California gold camps. He settled first in Virginia City, then moved eastward to Elko in 1869, where he became one of the town's first shopkeepers. In his small cabin near the Humboldt River, Hiram began drinking. Night after night, he spent the lonely hours sitting by his stove and getting drunk on whiskey.

One night in 1872, a ghost appeared to Hiram. "If you stick your hands in the stove and burn 'em off," the ghost said, "you'll have no more worries about drinking."

Hiram stared at the ghost through his alcohol-induced stupor. Yes, it seemed logical to him. Without hands he couldn't lift the bottle to pour the whiskey, or a glass to drink it from. Before thinking it through, he covered his hands with grease, opened the stove door, and stuck them in the fire. The pain was unbearable. As his hands turned to shriveled blackened stumps in the flames, Hiram cried out in pain. Rather than offer sympathy, the ghost turned from him and vanished into thin air.

Neighbors who heard the injured man's howls helped him get to the doctor. On seeing the extent of Hiram's injuries, the doctor had no choice. The only thing he could do was amputate both of Hiram's hands. From that moment on, Hiram Chase never took another drop of alcohol nor spoke of the ghost who'd told him to put his hands in the fire. Nor would he ask for charity. He continued operating his little store—right up to the time he died in the spring of 1905.

I Don't Believe in Ghosts, but...

*N*o one who is as interested in ghosts as I am is going to miss an opportunity to ask about hauntings. On a recent visit to Elko that had nothing to do with ghosts, we stopped in at one of our favorite Elko places to eat. While our server was speaking with another diner, I overheard her say that she was from Elko and "watched all the ghost shows."

That was my cue. When she returned to our table, I asked, "Do you know of any ghosts here in Elko?"

"Not really, but I think the kitchen is haunted," she said, motioning toward a swinging door.

"Why do you think so?" I asked.

"I've been grabbed a couple of times in there."

Before I could ask for details, another employee came to the table smiling. "Is she bothering you?" he asked.

"She wants to know if there are any ghosts in town," she said, motioning toward me.

He smiled at me. "I don't believe in ghosts, but I can tell you that the old Commercial Hotel on Idaho Street is haunted."

"Really?" I said. "What makes you say so?"

"The place used to be a boarding house—they say at least five people have been murdered in there. They say there are three ghosts. There's the lady who was cheating on her husband at the hotel. He came up to the second floor where she was staying and shot and killed her and her lover. Then he killed himself. The men wander the building. She walks up and down the hallway crying and moaning. My office was just down the hall from that room, and I can tell you that some weird things happened to me in that office. One night I was in there about midnight, and something touched my cheek. Icy cold it was. Another time I thought I saw her." He looked at me and shook his head. "That was a strange place, but again, I don't believe in ghosts."

Later I found out that the Commercial Hotel had indeed begun as the Humboldt Lodging House in 1869. In 1893, after a succession of owners, it was remodeled and became the Commercial Hotel. Over the years, different paranormal groups have investigated the hotel and found it indeed haunted. While it is said that many deaths occurred in the building, I found two: a death by natural causes in 1869 and the suicide death of John Coble, a friend of condemned lawman/killer Tom Horn.

Coble was distraught over personal problems when he walked into the Commercial Hotel on the morning of December 4, 1914. He calmly asked the clerk to borrow a pen and paper, wrote a brief note to his wife, then walked into the ladies' bathroom and shot himself.

Some of those who've investigated the hotel have received the name John, or Tom, during EVP sessions. A young investigator told of encountering a ghostly man that fit Coble's description. Thinking it might be him, she asked if he was unhappy with decisions he'd made in his life. Sobbing loudly, the ghost nodded. Before she could ask another question, the ghostly man turned and vanished into a nearby wall.

Aside from the ghosts, the Commercial Hotel holds an important place in Nevada history. The Commercial Hotel was the first place in Nevada to offer live entertainment in its casino lounge. This was during the early 1940s, and owner Newt Crumley was looking for a way to increase his gambling business when he came up with the idea to bring big names of the era to perform, thus keeping customers at the tables and the slots. The idea was a huge success. So huge, in fact, that Las Vegas and Reno soon followed suit. The rest is gambling and showbiz history.

As of this writing, the hotel is closed.

Southern Nevada

Las Vegas

Since the dawning of the twenty-first century, Las Vegas has grown to become a very large city, a 24/7 city where nothing ever closes. There is always something to do and something to see here. Someone once said that if you can't find it in Las Vegas, it doesn't exist. And that includes ghosts, and it's probably true. Las Vegas long ago supplanted Hollywood as the entertainment capital of the world, so it's not surprising that many of the city's ghosts are stars, or in the case of mobster Bugsy Siegel, members of the underworld.

Bugsy

Las Vegas became a city in 1905. That was long before gangster Benjamin Bugsy Siegel came to town. Because of his role in the city's gaming history, Bugsy Siegel is considered the father of modern Las Vegas. The debonair Bugsy drove to Las Vegas in the early 1940s, took one look at Nevada's legalized gambling, and decided that he and his pals could make a pile of money here on the edge of the Mojave Desert—all legally. After persuading his bosses of this, he was put in charge of overseeing the building and operations of a casino that he called the Flamingo.

His vision of the riches that waited in the legal gambling world was spot on. He just hadn't realized that it might take some time for the Flamingo to start paying off. He also hadn't factored in the impatience of his bosses, the money people. They wanted theirs pronto. And Bugsy couldn't deliver. So the inevitable happened. Bugsy was killed in Beverly Hills on June 20, 1947—an unsolved crime. But who's kidding who? Everyone knew it was Bugsy's bosses who'd ordered the hit on the handsome gangster.

Most people would leave it there. But not the ghostly Bugsy; he returned to Las Vegas and his beloved Flamingo Hotel. Here he took up residence in his former penthouse. When the penthouse was demolished to make way for improvements to the hotel, Bugsy relocated to other locations throughout the property, mainly the wedding chapel and the wildlife habitat. He was also spotted on a Las Vegas tour bus—playing the tourist and reliving happier times before he fell into disfavor with his bosses.

MGM Grand Las Vegas

Built in 1973, the MGM Grand Hotel Casino towered over other casino hotels with its twenty-six stories and signaled an era never before seen in Las Vegas. Here was a dazzling display of glamour, top-name entertainment, and sophistication. It all ended in the early morning hours of November 21, 1980, six days before Thanksgiving.

The MGM Grand Hotel fire would be the worst disaster in Nevada's history, and one of the worst hotel fires in the world. Of the over five thousand people in the MGM Grand Hotel on that fateful morning in November, 650 were injured enough to seek medical attention. Eighty-seven perished in the fire.

The fire started while many of the hotel's guests slept. The result of faulty wiring that ignited a fire in the wall of the ground floor deli, the flames moved swiftly. Even as two employees tried desperately to contain it, the fire was out of control within minutes. The fast-moving flames spread through the casino floor. Flammable material such as plastic molding, carpeting, and wallpaper used in the hotel's construction was ignited and melted, releasing toxic fumes into the air. Those who were working and gambling in the ground floor casino didn't have a chance; they were overcome by the fumes and died where they stood.

Up in the tower rooms, guests had no idea of the danger until it was too late. Flames had engulfed the ground floor and were shooting upward. The thick black smoke rose up through the building's heating and air-conditioning system. Alerted by the drone of several helicopters hovering around the building and the unmistakable smell, guests called the hotel front desk. But that area had fallen to the flames, and there was no one left to answer their calls. Panic stricken, they turned on their televisions to the horror of what was happening.

As panic set in, they ran into the halls and were overcome by the smoke. Frightened and disoriented, one person leapt from the north side of the tower to the parking lot far below. A lucky few would manage to escape death by making their way through the blinding smoke and noxious fumes to the rooftop where firemen and rescuers had stacked bodies for transport by helicopters. The dead would be taken to the parking lot for further identification; the injured would be transported to local hospitals. In all, it would be four hours before the building was evacuated.

Today the state of Nevada has some of the strictest fire prevention building code laws in the United Sates. After lawsuits totaling more than $200 million, the burned-out MGM Grand was sold, demolished, and transformed into Bally's Las Vegas. And it is haunted.

Most paranormal experts will tell you that ghostly activity is often the result of great tragedy and sudden, unexpected death. The tragedy that took place on this spot in 1980 is no exception.

Unexplained weeping and screaming have been reported in the upper-floor hallways. In certain areas of the hotel, disoriented apparitions have been encountered. Down on the casino floor, ghosts dressed in 1970s attire wander among the living. Most people never even see them. Those who do say the ghosts seem agitated and angry.

Then there is that service elevator that no employee wants to take a ride in. Is it haunted? Some say it isn't. Others don't want to go anywhere near it.

At the Luxor

*T*he largest two pyramids in the world are located at Giza. And the third—well, that pyramid is located right here in Las Vegas, the Luxor Hotel that was built in 1993.

Many believe the Luxor is cursed for two reasons: its large sphinx faces eastward instead of westward, and the large light atop the pyramid, called the sky beam, has not been capped. Capping the light, some say, will bring good luck to the city. Speaking of the sky beam, legend has it that it was visible to astronauts as their space capsules circled the earth. That may or may not be the case. But airline pilots report seeing it.

Since we're here in Las Vegas on a ghost quest, I'll tell you that the thirty-story-tall Luxor is rumored to be one of the most haunted places on the Strip. Given the inordinate number of deaths, both suicide and murder, that have occurred here in the pyramid, that's easy to see. From the beginning when a workman fell to his death during its construction, there have been several deaths connected to the Luxor, including the very location it sits upon.

A long-held Las Vegas tale has it that back in the day when the mob ruled Las Vegas, this location was a favorite dumping ground for hit men wanting to dispose of their victims quickly. The ghostly man in a brown suit who wanders the hallways of the upper floors has been seen by many people. Before you ask, he's been seen by those who've had a few cocktails and those who haven't partaken. He appears to be a businessman and is believed to be the victim of an early hit. If you should encounter him, know that he never says a word. He just wanders past as if asking himself what happened.

A twist on the old hag syndrome, sleep paralysis, is the beautiful blonde ghost who's appeared before countless Luxor patrons. Is she a former showgirl, perhaps? Or was she a long-legged cigarette girl from the days when women were hired to don skimpy costumes and saunter through the casino selling cigarettes, gum, and candy? Whoever she was, don't get too comfortable with her.

If she is in your room, chances are you won't be sleeping very well. She isn't the ghostly old hag, and you won't experience sleep paralysis, but you just might wake up with the sensation of someone trying to choke you. No, it isn't the garlic-laden fettuccini you had for dinner that haunts you. It's the blonde. And for whatever reason, she is serious about keeping you awake. Sure, you can complain to the desk. They've heard it all before. But this is Las Vegas, and they will maintain an icy professionalism through the entire conversation.

There is a ghostly young lady who is said to wander the hallway of a certain floor. I believe she is a young prostitute who was choked to death in a room at the Luxor in 1997. Her name was Sara. If you should encounter her, remember that.

According to some, one particular room is haunted by a noisy ghost who's said to exist on a certain time schedule. Don't worry, he never appears to guests. However, he is dead set against sleeping in. No pun intended. So go ahead, party all night if you must—this is Las Vegas, after all. But be prepared. Regardless of what time you call it a night, this ghost will wake you up at 8:30 in the morning with loud boisterous noise. Alert security and complain. They know what is going on; nonetheless, someone will come to check on your room. No source for the noise will ever be found. You can bet on it!

Elvis Was Here, There, and Everywhere

*W*ith the recent Elvis movie starring Austin Butler, there has been a renewed interest in Elvis Presley. Some may say those words are sacrilege, but the popularity of celebrities both dead and alive waxes and wanes. And every year the lineup of Elvis impersonators dwindles. But thankfully his ghost is still appearing in Las Vegas, the city that was so special to him.

Likewise, Elvis was special to Las Vegas. It was here in 1967 that the King of Rock and Roll married the beautiful Priscilla Beaulieu in a lavish wedding ceremony at the old Aladdin Hotel. Photos of the bride and groom are all over the internet. There is Priscilla of the bouffant hair and cat-eye kohl makeup, and Elvis in yesterday's cool hairstyle.

Two years later, Elvis made a comeback. He returned to Las Vegas set to appear at the International Hotel. It had been eight years since he'd performed before a live audience; the stakes were high. He needed to revive a career that had slowed with his stint in the army and the so-called British invasion of the music scene. But this was Elvis—and he was magic to those who remembered the younger, livelier Elvis. He gave them what they wanted. And the Las Vegas run was a success. He was in demand and back on top of his game.

The ghostly Elvis has been spotted at locations across Las Vegas. Recently one of his old party spots, the Hartland Mansion at the corner of Charleston Boulevard and Sixth Street, was demolished to make way for progress. The Hartland was built in 1940 and was touted as the largest private residence in Las Vegas. All the big names stayed and partied here, especially Elvis. And this is probably why his ghost was seen countless times throughout the mansion.

Longtime Las Vegas entertainer Robert George Allen and I formed a friendship out of a shared interest in the paranormal, particularly ghosts. As the creator of the popular Las Vegas Ghost

Tour, Robert had gathered many local Vegas ghost stories. One of my favorites was of his experience with the ghostly Elvis at the Hartland Mansion.

> This was sometime in the early nineties. Elvis had been dead for years. I was at a party at the Hartland; a lot of big names were there. I looked across the room and saw Elvis's doppelgänger. I'm not kidding; he looked just like the guy. I remember thinking that he was the perfect Elvis impersonator. I wanted to hear how well he did the voice, so I moved closer to where he stood, surrounded by a small group of people. I was no more than twenty or so feet from him. From that distance I could see that he was about the same age as Elvis and definitely had all the mannerisms. When he laughed, it was Elvis's laugh. When he spoke—he had Elvis's voice down pat. Obviously he'd put some serious study into Elvis.
>
> I walked closer to him ready to say, "I've got to hand it to you, you're one of the best Elvis impersonators I've ever seen."
>
> The words never came. When I got closer to him, the room suddenly fell silent and cold as if I'd stepped into a refrigerator—just like that, he was gone, and so were the people who'd been talking with him. I was in some sort of haze, until I figured it out. That guy was Elvis. Well, Elvis's ghost anyway.

The most famous person to see the ghostly Elvis in Las Vegas was Mr. Las Vegas himself, Wayne Newton. In his 1989 autobiography, *Once Before I Go*, the singer told of seeing Elvis in the balcony during one of his performances.

I realize there are people who completely disagree with me about the ghostly Elvis haunting Las Vegas. These are also the people who know full well that Elvis is alive and well and enjoying the good life somewhere on an island in the South Pacific. And all I've got to say about that is—I hope he hasn't forgotten his sunscreen.

Zak Bagans's The Haunted Museum

On his popular television show *Ghost Adventures*, Zak Bagans has been seeking out ghosts and other strange paranormal phenomena for several years. Driven by his passion for the subject matter, Zak began amassing a large collection of macabre memorabilia and opened his haunted museum on Charleston Boulevard on April 2, 2016.

With things like the murderous Ed Gein's cauldron, Charles Mansion's ashes, Bella Lugosi's mirror, and the devil's rocking chair, there's bound to be something strange lurking in the eleven-thousand-square-foot house that was built in 1938.

Staff have reported encountering some weird things, including the ghostly man in a black cowl and cape that walks through closed doors and calmly wanders through the museum. Visitors to the museum have seen him as well. The question is, is the man attached to the house, or was he attached to one of the many objects Zak has here at the museum? Some say there is a definite dark vibe at the museum; some visitors have even suffered headaches and nosebleeds during their tours. No one knows what dark paranormal energy might appear or what might happen; this is why visitors to the museum must sign a release statement.

Recently YouTube stars Sam Golbach and Colby Scherer, along with some of their friends, did an episode of their show *Sam and Colby* in the museum after hours. Clearly the place that houses so many unusual artifacts with dark histories is haunted. And who better to stir up the ghosts than Sam and Colby?

My own story of the museum takes place before it was opened. I was there and looking through the building with Zak when I spotted a nice wooden chest. I reached to touch it when Zak pulled me away, saying, "Don't touch that; it's cursed!"

That was enough for me. I didn't want to go anywhere near that chest again. Do you blame me?

Liberace

*T*he flamboyant celebrity was larger than life—and apparently larger than death as well. When viewed from the outside, his home in a Las Vegas middle-class neighborhood on Shirley Avenue wasn't what you might consider posh. Once inside, things were altogether different. The showman had designed his home to suit is colorful personality. With a piano-shaped swimming pool, mirrors and ornate trappings everywhere, a king-size bathtub, and a replica of the Sistine Chapel ceiling in his boudoir, Liberace put his stamp on the middle-class house.

Several years ago, I had the opportunity to visit the home with my mother, who lives in Las Vegas. Mama happily agreed to drive us to Shirley Avenue *if*, and she stressed *if*, the ghost of Liberace didn't bother her.

"You were a big fan. Why would he bother you?" I asked.

"Yes, but now that he's dead, I don't want anything to do with him," she said petulantly.

"If his ghost shows up, I swear—I'll leave and you will have to walk home."

And that was not a pleasant prospect, considering this was summer and the temperatures were well over a hundred degrees.

In desperation, I decided to do a little name-dropping.

"Listen, Lee," I said to myself. "I'm calling you Lee because we have a couple of mutual friends, Robert Allen and Dixie Dooley, okay? My mom and I are coming to see your house, and I am asking you to please not scare Mama."

Her fears allayed, Mama drove us across town and excitedly jumped out of the car. She couldn't wait to get inside Liberace's home. The caretaker greeted us at the door and began showing me around while Mama lagged behind. Awestruck by the bedroom and bathroom with all the mirrors, I pulled out my camera and started taking photos. Despite the ceiling that was painted in the style of the Sistine Chapel and the oversized bathtub with its gold fixtures, I felt that these two rooms were where the ghostly Liberace would probably be spending most of his time.

Where was Mama, I wondered. Why hadn't she joined us?

Retracing my steps, I found her in the foyer by the fountain, looking very perplexed.

"What's wrong?" I asked.

"I think Liberace was telling me he is still here," she said. "I wasn't standing very close to the fountain when I glanced up and noticed a stream of silvery blue water spiraling down from the ceiling. I told myself to be careful not to slip and fall in the water that was puddling on the marble floor. I was wondering how on earth that water was coming down from the ceiling, and how it was connected to the water fountain. Then I looked up, and there was no water and no stream. I looked at the floor, and the puddle of water was gone. I looked up and saw the blue painting of Liberace—and it was exactly where the water was coming from."

I silently acknowledged Liberace and thanked him for not scaring Mama, and we continued our tour. I've told this story many times over the years, but it's been only recently that Mama has agreed to let me say that she was the woman who saw water coming from Liberace's ceiling.

In 2013 a fan of Liberace's purchased the home from foreclosure and began extensive renovations. In 2016, the Clark County Board of Commissioners gave Liberace's home a historical designation. This was the first such designation for a residential building in the state of Nevada.

Haunted Mansion

*P*icture this: a million-dollar-plus palatial mansion with five bed-rooms, five bathrooms, a porte cochere, and a sparkling pool, on nearly an acre of prime Las Vegas real estate, surrounded by tall stately palm trees. Is there a problem? Not unless you count the hateful ghosts who are supposed to be haunting this exquisite home.

The mansion was built in 1959, and rumor has it that it belonged to a high-placed mob figure. That's possible, since these were the days when the mob ruled Las Vegas. And according to stories, some very terrible things went on in the home during that time. This released so much negative energy into the building that it continues to haunt and harass anyone who lives there.

Although there is a tremendous amount of ghostly hype sur-rounding this mansion, it doesn't look like anyone's idea of a haunted house. Nonetheless, this is one of those places, for all its exquisite remodeling, that people move into and out of in a hurry. Everyone seems to have had different experiences. Some who've lived here have been confronted by a dark humanlike mass; oth-ers have been pushed or shoved even in broad daylight. Dishes being tossed around the dining room and disembodied voices that threaten physical violence and even death are some of the ghostly occurrences reported to have happened here.

All who've experience the house agree that the feelings they have while here in this mansion are negative and oppressive. Now for the good news—the Las Vegas real estate market is booming, and the mansion is on the market at a really good price—practically a steal for just the right buyer.

Nelson and the Ghosts of El Dorado Canyon

In the late 1700s, Spanish explorers discovered gold in a canyon on the present-day Colorado River. They called this place El Dorado. A hundred years later, and long before Nevada became a state, traders and merchants were traveling the seven-hundred-mile Viejo Sendero Español (the Old Spanish Trail) trade route between Santa Fe, New Mexico, and Los Angeles. The trail had been laid out as early as the 1600s by the Spanish explorers in the region.

In 1859, about the same time that the silver rush began in Virginia City, two rich gold veins were discovered here in the El Dorado Canyon. A town named after Charles Nelson was formed here on the banks of the Colorado River. Among Native Americans, there was much anger and resentment against the colonizers who had come here to take their land. In 1891, his anger at a fever pitch, a Native American named Avote went on a rampage, slaughtering everyone he encountered. When he came to the settlement of Nelson namesake Charles Nelson, he killed the man without a second thought.

Hundreds of people continued to pour into the area, seeking their share of the gold, one way or the other. Among these newcomers were lawless and brutal men, some who had either fought in or deserted during the Civil War. Violence and bloodshed were a daily occurrence.

The name given to one of the largest mines in the canyon, Techatticup, was formed of two Paiute words meaning "hungry" and "bread." Besides being the largest, the Techatticup Mine was also the most productive mine in the canyon, founded before Nevada became a state. After Nevada gained statehood in 1864, the Techatticup Mine was within the Arizona Territory because of state boundaries. In 1869, the boundaries were redrawn, and the land was given to Nevada. Good thing; otherwise Las Vegas would be in Arizona.

The Techatticup Mine was the scene of an unsolved murder on January 21, 1919, when Maude Douglas, the wife of Irvin Douglas, was shot to death in their cabin at the mine. It was believed that a Native American outlaw known as Queho was responsible. Queho killed so many people during his lifetime that he is known as Nevada's first mass murderer.

Today a small monument marks the location of Maude Douglas's senseless murder. Some have seen the ghostly woman who wanders this area as well. Dressed in attire of the early twentieth century, she is believed to be the ghostly Maude Douglas. The specter never says a word—just stares into the distance as if trying to remember something.

The Techatticup Mine would continue to produce well into the 1940s. During that time, the mine would produce more than $250 million worth of gold and silver. Of course it was not the only mine in El Dorado Canyon. This brings us to John Nash, a thoroughly despicable hombre, who came to the canyon with big ideas—none of which were honest and aboveboard. He decided that he would jump George Hearst's Queen City claim to get what he wanted. In order to carry out his plans, he hired three partners, promising to pay them handsomely for their part in his scheme. The men were as dishonest as Nash and, expecting a larger windfall when Nash struck it rich, they agreed to help him carry out his plan. But they hadn't figured on Nash's duplicity.

Promising an even bigger share of the gold, he tricked the men into killing one another. Two of them died of strychnine poisoning; the third man, Jim Jones, was shot to death by the leader of a posse that was chasing him. Nash could now rest easy. His partners were all dead, and the money was his. He was a wealthy man. But even as he made plans on how he would spend all that money, a vengeful ghost was watching him. And he was about to make certain that John Nash's plan didn't work out the way he hoped it would. The ghost of Jim Jones made his appearance one morning and began to follow Nash wherever he went.

Nash tried to put it off to being overly tired, imagination, and perhaps too much whiskey. But the ghostly Jim Jones wasn't having that. He loudly harangued Nash for being the evil-hearted man that he was. This continued every day as Nash went about his work, and every evening when he returned to his cabin exhausted from the day's work.

Overwhelmed by guilt, John Nash was not able to withstand the torment from Jones. No matter where he went, there was Jones, reminding him of what he'd done. No matter how he tried to reason with the ghostly Jim Jones, the torment continued. Day by day, Nash slowly went insane, dying a miserable death.

He hasn't gone far, though. His anguished screams echo through the canyon as his ghost tries desperately to avoid Jim Jones and keep all the gold for himself. In this, he has a right to be concerned. They say that the ghostly Jim Jones is still there in Nelson as well. And he wanders in and out of the abandoned mines in search of John Nash, seeking to torment him into eternity.

Ghosts at Madame Tussauds

*W*elcome to the wax museum, where ghosts lurk among the wax likenesses of celebrities. The museum opened on the Strip in 1999 and was the first Madame Tussauds to be opened in the United States. Of course it was. Las Vegas has everything; where else would the iconic Madame Tussauds choose for its premier location?

So who was here first, the ghosts or the museum? Some believe the museum is haunted by ghosts of the former hotel/casino that stood on this spot—the old Sands Hotel. And we're being technical; Madame Tussauds is where the Sands' Copa Room was located. And with nothing left of their old pied-à-terre, the ghostly Rat Pack—that is, Frank Sinatra, Dean Martin, and Sammy Davis Jr.—have chosen to hang around Madame Tussauds, entertaining an equally ghostly nightclub audience. With the cost of cover charges going up, they may be on to something.

That is one theory. There are others.

Stoney

In Las Vegas, a town where things are larger than life and death, there is the ghostly Stoney, the elephant who roams the Craig Road Pet Cemetery. The glowing pachyderm has been seen many times as he wanders through the cemetery when most of the world, everywhere else, is sleeping. If size matters, know this—Stoney just may be the largest ghost in Nevada. In this place where the beloved pets of the famous rest, Stoney's story is probably the saddest of all that are told here at the Craig Road Pet Cemetery.

At first glance, it might have seemed as if good fortune had put Stoney the bull elephant on the path to stardom when he was chosen to perform in an act called the "Winds of the Gods" at the Luxor Hotel Casino. But his luck was short-lived. Stoney missed his footing and broke a hind leg during a performance, cutting short his show-room career. After a thorough examination, vets realized that this was a serious injury and nothing could be done for the elephant. Consequently, he died at the age of twenty-two years. His headstone features an elephant engraving and reads simply, "In loving memory of Stoney a Gentle Giant."

Thankfully Stoney's bad luck didn't followed him to the grave; those who've seen him say the ghostly Stoney seems happy and content and is enjoying the good life in the afterlife at the pet cemetery.

Mr. Petrie at the Las Vegas Academy of the Arts

With more than two million people living in Las Vegas today, it's hard to believe that in 1931 the city's population was about five and a half thousand. Construction of the Hoover Dam would change that as more people came to Las Vegas looking for work.

The city was twenty-six years old in 1931, and a new school was needed. That new high school was Las Vegas High School. And it was built in an area that many considered to be the outskirts of town—it would remain the first and only high school in Las Vegas until the mid-1950s.

Las Vegas High School was listed on the National Register of Historic Places in 1986. And in 1994, it was converted to the Las Vegas Academy of the Arts. Among the academy's most famous alumni are Matthew Gray Gubler and Julianne Hough. Like many such places, there is a ghost in residence here at the Las Vegas Academy of the Arts. He is known affectionately as Mr. Petrie, and there are countless stories as to who he is and why he is haunting the academy.

One tale has Mr. Petrie as a former teacher at the old Las Vegas High School. Another has him a former student of the high school who refused to stop going to class even after death. Still another story has Mr. Petrie as an elderly man who died of a horrendous fire in his home near the school. Whoever he was in life, the name, Mr. Petrie, has stuck. And he is solidly ensconced here at the academy; students have been talking about Mr. Petrie since Las Vegas High School's earliest days.

For those who demand proof, consult the Las Vegas High School's 1968 yearbook. As the story goes, a photo of the ghostly Mr. Petrie appears in that yearbook. I've not seen it, so I cannot say one way or the other. But I can tell you that Mr. Petrie prefers spending time in the auditorium, where he is responsible for flickering lights (a favorite of ghosts), eerie laughter, icy breezes, and unexplained footsteps.

According to some, he can show up anytime, day or night. And he has been known to startle students by making a sudden appearance as a shadowy figure.

Tour Guide Ghost

*T*his story gave me chills when I first heard it because the ghost involved was a friend of mine. But then I thought, who would love starring in his own ghost tale more than Robert? His name was Robert Allen, and he loved nothing better than entertaining and being the center of attention. He died two days before Halloween, leaving his popular Haunted Las Vegas Ghost Tour in someone else's hands. The show, as they say, must go on. And it did—night after night.

Then came that cold and windy January night when several people who'd known Robert happened to be on board the bus as it slowly made its way down a dark neighborhood street. Suddenly someone gasped, interrupting the tour guide's spiel.

"Look! Look out the window. That's Robert walking down the street."

As they stared through the window, most of them agreed. It was Robert, and he appeared much as he always had in his long black coat and top hat. He seemed thoroughly confused, as if he was wondering why the bus had driven off and left him.

"Turn around!" someone insisted. "Go back and make sure it's Robert."

The tour guide nodded his agreement, knowing it didn't make sense. That couldn't possibly have been Robert. He had been dead for several months now. Still, the driver dutifully turned the bus around and drove back down the street—the empty street. There was no sign of anyone, anywhere. Those who'd seem him swore up and down they'd seen the ghostly Robert wandering along the street.

Much later, the tour guide assured himself that there was no way they'd seen Robert Allen—unless . . .

Ghosts on Blue Diamond Road Route 160

Blue Diamond Road is a fifty-mile length of highway known to locals at the Highway of Death. There's a good reason for this. Numerous automobile fatalities have taken place on this stretch of roadway between Las Vegas and Pahrump. Some people refuse to drive Blue Diamond Road, believing it is cursed by all the deaths that have occurred here.

Then, too, there are the ghosts who roam this highway. Motorists have told of an elderly couple that walks along the roadway, vanishing into the desert air as your car passes by them, and of a glowing woman who wanders aimlessly down the middle of the road in the early morning hours just before the sun comes up. Of course you will swerve to avoid her. But not to worry, she vanishes the moment your car approaches. There is also an elderly couple that appears along the roadway on full moon nights. You might think they are lost; you might even stop to offer them help. They are in no need of earthly help. And they will demonstrate this by dissolving into nothingness the moment you stop your car.

The most famous person to die here on Blue Diamond Road was retired porn star Anna Malle (Anna Hotop-Stout). Malle died when an oncoming vehicle plowed into the car she was riding in. Malle wasn't wearing a seatbelt and joined the ranks of those who've died here on the Highway of Death.

Hoover Dam Ghosts

It took four years to build Boulder Dam, from 1931 to 1935. During its construction, more than a hundred men lost their lives due to heatstroke or accident. The most coincidental loss of life here are the deaths of John Gregory Tierney and his son Patrick. On December 20, 1921, John was a member of a surveying crew that got caught in a flash flood on the Colorado River. Tierney became the second man to die while working on the Boulder Dam project when he fell from his boat and disappeared into the water.

Fourteen years later, on the same date, December 20, his son Patrick became the last man to die on the Boulder Dam project when he fell to his death from one of the two intake towers.

From its beginning, the dam was called Boulder Dam. It wasn't until 1947 that the name Hoover Dam was officially restored. A tale that's as old as the dam itself is that no rescue attempt was made whenever a man fell to his death. Instead his body was covered over with cement and the work continued. Historians and dam experts are quick to point out that this is just an urban legend.

What isn't an urban legend is that many people have chosen to jump to their deaths here at Hoover Dam. Sadly, their ghosts remain here to reenact their terrible decision. The ghostly dam worker has been appearing to people in the elevator and at certain workstations for many years. There is a noticeable drop in temperature whenever he is around.

Boulder City

Located about twenty-five miles from Las Vegas in one direction and Boulder Dam in the other, Boulder City calls itself the "Best City by a Dam Site." It is unique in Nevada as being only one of two cities that do not permit gambling within city limits. This is because the US government founded the town for workers on the dam. Neither gambling nor alcohol was permitted. This lasted until the town was incorporated in 1960 and the ban on alcohol was lifted.

El Dorado Valley Pet Cemetery

Known unofficially for years as the Boulder Pet Cemetery, the El Dorado Valley Pet Cemetery is listed on the Find a Grave website. The cemetery is located in the desert about eight miles outside of Boulder City. For the past several years, hundreds of pet owners have buried their cherished pets here, even though it is technically illegal to do so.

Among those resting here is the big ghostly white cat that is said to wander the cemetery after dark. Perhaps as a way of offering comfort, this kitty is usually encountered by recently bereaved pet owners. After choosing who he/she will approach, the cat happily saunters up to that person, tail held high and purring loudly.

Where did you come from out here in the middle of the desert? Ask if you must. You'll get your answer if you should reach down to stroke the kitty—and notice there is nothing but air.

Boulder Dam Hotel

The Boulder Dam Hotel was built in 1933 to accommodate visitors to the Boulder Dam. The hotel soon became popular with Hollywood celebrities and dignitaries. The list of stars who have slept at the hotel reads like an early-day Hollywood Who's Who: Boris Karloff, Will Rogers, Bette Davis, Henry Fonda, and Shirley Temple are but a few.

While recuperating from his 1943 private plane crash at nearby Lake Mead, Howard Hughes chose to stay at the Boulder Dam Hotel. Years later the reclusive billionaire would choose to stay at the Desert Inn in Las Vegas while buying up most of the casinos in town.

But here at the Boulder Dam Hotel in 1943, he didn't keep quite a low profile. There are rumored to be several ghosts here at the hotel, but Howard Hughes is not one of them. Employees have told of hearing laughter and music in the ballroom when it is empty and no one is about. There is also an area of the hotel where the aroma of cigar smoke is often detected. I can attest to this phenomenon.

On a rainy fall day, my mother and I visited Boulder City to see the Boulder Dam Hotel and its museum. As I waited for her outside the ladies' room door, I noticed cigar smoke curling within a few feet of me. I inhaled. Yes, it was cigar smoke. I walked down the hall to the lobby and looked at the grand piano. No one was anywhere to be seen. The aroma was unmistakable, but I realized that whoever was smoking the cigar didn't exist on this earthly plane.

About that time my mother joined me. "It's the strangest thing," she said. "When I came out, I heard the most beautiful piano music. I felt like someone was guiding me toward the music, and there's the piano. But no one is playing."

We put it down to a ghost and continued our tour of the hotel and the museum.

The lobby is not the only area where ghosts hang out. According to some, the basement of the hotel is haunted by at least two ghosts. Unlike the former night clerk, who is the most popular ghost in residence, they are rarely seen. You may see the night clerk anywhere in the Boulder Dam Hotel. He likes to get around and has been spotted throughout the building. Those who've seen him say he always nods happily in acknowledgment when he realizes he's been noticed. Apparently the affable ghost enjoys the job so much he's decided to stay on indefinitely.

And for those who want to sleep in a room with ghostly activity, or avoid it, remember rooms 209 and 219. They are said to be the hotel's haunted rooms.

Lost City Ghosts

*T*his area in Southern Nevada is one of the state's most intriguing locations. The mysterious ghosts of Nevada's Lost City are, without a doubt, the oldest ghosts in the state. Brothers Fay and John Perkins discovered the remnants of a lost civilization while prospecting for gold nearly a hundred years ago.

When notified of the Perkins's find, Governor James Scrugham, a former engineer, realized the importance of such a discovery and sought help from outside sources in excavating the area. Worldwide attention was soon focused on Nevada and its Lost City, estimated to be seven thousand years old. During the first excavations, skeletons were discovered buried in the floors and walls of communal houses, in addition to tools and other household items.

The site known as Pueblo Grande de Nevada was nearly six miles square, stirring the imagination of scientists and scholars alike. Why had the Ancestral Puebloan people left their homes and precious belongings behind? Where had they gone? Those are questions that archaeologists hoped to answer.

You'll find answers and artifacts at the Lost City Museum in Overton. The museum's exhibits include artifacts like pottery, shells, and jewelry from the Pueblo Grande de Nevada. According to some, there are ghosts lurking here as well. A ghostly man is said to wander the museum. He is from a much more modern time than the two ghosts who've been seen outside the museum building near the reconstructed pueblos. Listen! Some claim it is nothing but the wind. But those who've heard it say that this is the sound of ghosts from ancient times singing and chanting.

Lake Mead and the Underwater Ghost Towns

*T*here are ghost towns, and then there are ghost towns. St. Thomas is a ghost town that is submerged by the waters of Lake Mead during non-drought years. As of this writing, Nevada is experiencing a drought that has caused the waters of the manmade Lake Mead to recede. This has made St. Thomas visible once again. Also visible from time to time is the ghostly young lady in white who walks among the ruins of the old ghost town.

With the completion of Hoover Dam in 1935, waters from the Colorado River began spilling over and filling Lake Mead. The towns of St. Thomas, Callville, and Rioville were given word that their towns were doomed and would soon be beneath the waters of Lake Mead. Everyone would have to leave. This included the dead. All the graves in the St. Thomas cemetery would need to be moved. Once the laborious task was completed, the graves were relocated to Mead Lake Cemetery in Overton. Today, the cemetery is called St. Thomas Memorial Cemetery. On June 11, 1938, the water rushed in, covering St. Thomas, Callville, Rioville, and the Pueblo Grande de Nevada. The creation of Lake Mead was complete.

Lake Mead is one of the largest reservoirs in the United States and the sixth most-visited place in the National Park System. It is also a location where ghosts are said to walk as shadowy figures that briefly appear at dusk, staying until the wee hours of the morning when the desert is still. Many believe that they are the ghosts of those who died here at Lake Mead, or those who vanished here without a trace.

They could also be the lonely ghosts of St. Thomas, those whose graves were disturbed in order to make way for the dam and the lake. Ghost researchers will tell you that it is never a good thing to disturb a grave, even for a good cause such as bringing water to a drought-stricken desert region.

Speaking of the drought, with Lake Mead's low water levels, a barrel containing a gun and the remains of a man was discovered. He died sometime between the 1970s and 1980s. Clearly, the man didn't die of natural causes. There is the assumption that he was the victim of a mob hit—and that may or may not be the truth. More human remains have been discovered here as the drought continues to cause Lake Mead's levels to drop.

Whiskey Pete

*O*ur next story takes place in Primm, a small unincorporated community of approximately 450. Located forty-four miles south of Las Vegas, Primm was originally known as Stateline because it is at the California-Nevada state line. But there was a small problem with this name. There was already a Stateline at Lake Tahoe in Northern Nevada. A name change was in order.

Since 1996, the town has been known as Primm in honor of Ernest Jay Primm, an early-day developer of the region. Mr. Primm would no doubt be very proud of what his family has achieved here; there are three large hotel casinos in Primm: Primm Valley Resort, Buffalo Bill's, and Whiskey Pete's, where the ghostly action begins.

The name Whiskey Pete is not the product of some slick ad campaign. You see, there really was a Whiskey Pete. He was Whiskey Pete McIntyre, a miner who ran a small gas station during Prohibition at the site of the hotel casino that bears his name. Times were hard, and Pete wasn't making the money he'd hoped to make—so he turned to producing and selling bootleg liquor at the gas station.

The money, and the cars, was rolling in. Even though Pete had found a need and was filling it, he still had the reputation of being a crotchety old man who partook too often of his own homebrewed whiskey, lacked patience, and was short a few social graces. Customers often complained about his behavior, which included shooting at (and thankfully missing) them. The Automobile Club of Southern California declared Pete a menace to the safety and well-being of travelers.

And yet, Pete McIntyre had his share of friends. When he died in 1934, Pete really put them to the test; on his deathbed, he was quoted as making a request: "Bury me up on the hill, standing up facing the valley, so I can see all those sons of bitches goin' by."

And according to a 1934 article in the *Cloudburst*, Pete's friends did just that.

> Whiskey Pete is dead and planted as he wished, feet first in a six-foot hole blasted by dynamite in the limestone cliff, behind his homestead at Stateline Station.
>
> At his wake irreverent ones suggested that he must have died of chagrin because repeal had removed his only incentive to go on living. And in their cups they toasted his pledge to hijack the devil out of hell.

So there, legend had it, Whiskey Pete McIntyre stood overlooking Arrowhead Highway, which today is known as I-15. And he might have rested here forever, if not for progress and that day in 1994.

A construction crew was working on an overpass bridge that would connect Whiskey Pete's to Buffalo Bill's hotel casino when they discovered Pete's grave. Describing Pete's remains, one member of the crew told the *Las Vegas Review-Journal*:

> It was just a skeleton really. . . . He still had dentures in his mouth. He still had a little hair left on his head.
>
> The Tractor caught the edge of the box and the skull popped out. There was Whiskey Pete staring at us.

It was decided that Pete's remains would be reburied in an undisclosed location on the property and progress could resume.

According to some, Whiskey Pete's remains were buried a short distance away in the same cave where he had once made his illegal liquor. And thus, Pete was left to rest in peace, once again.

Only he wasn't. You know what they say about disturbing someone's final resting place. It's true. One of the surest ways to guarantee that you will have a ghost at your location is to disturb the grave of someone associated with that location. We see it time and again in the paranormal.

So it comes as no surprise that about the same time Whiskey Pete's remains were unearthed, a ghostly old man began appearing to people in the parking lot and in the casino. There, he watches players intently. A woman who described her encounter with Pete in the parking lot said that he was an elderly man wearing overalls and a checkered shirt. He didn't say a word, just smiled and nodded at her as he approached. It wasn't until he vanished into thin air that she realized the old man was a ghost.

Gamblers are superstitious; that's a given. There is a woman who claimed that the ghostly Whiskey Pete helped her win a big jackpot when he pointed her to a different slot machine from the one she was playing. She'd already lost a pail full of coins and had nothing to lose. Why not take the old man's advice? She did. As it turned out, she was a big winner.

Please don't waste your time trying to tell her that there is no such thing as ghosts.

Goodsprings Ghosts

*L*ocated about forty miles southwest of Las Vegas, Goodsprings is a world apart. There may not be the glamour of Las Vegas, but there are ghosts. And that's why we've come.

Goodsprings' boom began with World War I. It was 1914, and more than thirty mines were operating here. With zinc and copper in high demand, the prices of these metals soared, and that was a good thing for Goodsprings. With mining, suddenly there were people and businesses and money in town. But just like other Nevada boomtowns, the end came as quickly as it had begun. And many of Goodsprings, residents packed up and left.

Proof of early-day mining activity is a scattering of old cabins, a few buildings, and rusted-out mining implements; these are about the only sign of the boom that once took place here.

Pioneer Saloon

*T*he Pioneer Saloon is probably the most famous haunted place in Goodsprings. Built in 1915 by local businessman George Arthur Fayle, the Pioneer Saloon is the gathering place for locals and those who come seeking local color. Things may have slowed down for Goodsprings, but you can count on one thing; someone at the Pioneer is usually more than willing to tell you about the ghosts here.

Movie stars Carole Lombard and Clark Gable are not the only ghosts to haunt the old saloon, but they are the most famous. The reason the two Hollywood hotshots of long ago are hanging out here is tragic. Lombard was returning to Hollywood from Indiana when her plane crashed on nearby Mount Potosi on January 15, 1942. Upon receiving word of the crash, Gable, Lombard's husband, rushed from Los Angeles to Goodsprings and awaited word of her fate at the Pioneer Saloon.

Days later, Lombard's body was recovered from Mount Potosi, and Gable headed back to Los Angeles to make funeral arrangements. Although the pair is said to haunt other locations, there are those who will tell you that Gable and Lombard have decided to stay on here at the Pioneer Saloon, enjoying the ambiance.

Several women have encountered a weeping blonde ghost in the ladies' bathroom that they believe is Carole Lombard. During a conversation with Lombard, one psychic medium asked her why she was crying. There was no reply. But when she was asked why she had chosen to stay here in the Nevada desert, the reply came quickly: "This is where Clark is."

Paul Coski is a ghost from a different era. His fate was sealed early on the morning of June 26, 1915, as a cool breeze wafted through the Pioneer Saloon. Coski was playing poker with Joe Armstrong, Roy Blood, Tom Lowe, and F. J. Schroeder. While the other men played an honest hand, Coski did not. When he was caught dealing himself a card from the bottom of the deck, the men demanded he split the pot and end the game.

Coski wanted all the money himself and refused. A fight broke out, and angry at being cheated, one of the men pulled a gun, shooting and killing Coski. The death was ruled justifiable, and Coski was quickly buried in the Goodsprings Cemetery. Apparently Coski isn't happy there and is not resting in peace. He has been seen numerous times in the Pioneer Saloon since that day in 1915. He's also been known to crowd those sitting at the bar, especially if they are ghost investigators with a lot of tech equipment.

The ghostly Coski seems to enjoy the ghost-hunting paraphernalia. So much so that he gets into the act; he is the ghost most paranormal investigators encounter during their investigations of the Pioneer Saloon. He's been heard on EVP saying, "The bullet's for me."

Rhyolite Ghosts

*B*ecause there is no light pollution out here in the middle of the desert, Rhyolite is a dream come true for photographers of the night sky. In fact, Rhyolite is probably Nevada's most photographed ghost town. Situated on the edge of the Mojave Desert in the Bullfrog Hills, Rhyolite is just 120 miles northwest of the famous Las Vegas Strip. Like so many other Nevada towns, Rhyolite grew to importance because of a rich ore discovery.

Shorty Harris and Ed Cross were two prospectors who teamed up and made a rich gold discovery (the Bullfrog Mining District) in the nearby hills in 1904. The rush to Rhyolite was on. A popular saying was, "You could go to bed broke and wake up a millionaire in Rhyolite." And every man and woman with a get-rich-quick dream wanted to come to Rhyolite. Within two years, the Las Vegas and Tonopah Railroad between Las Vegas and Goldfield began bringing passengers to and from the growing town. By 1907, nearly eight thousand people were living in Rhyolite, which had electric lights, many businesses, a bank, a hospital, a school, an opera house, and a stock exchange.

Said the *Tonopah Bonanza*, on July 28, 1906: "Rhyolite's Great Future: It will ultimately surpass the expectations of its warmest friends." But sadly Rhyolite's future was not great, and it didn't surpass expectations.

Rhyolite Takes Place among Ghost Towns
of the Booming West

Rhyolite, once a thriving center of the Bullfrog mining boom of fourteen years ago, has taken its place among the "ghost towns" of the west. (*Great Falls Tribune*, December 26, 1920)

Fourteen years after its discovery, the gold was exhausted, and the trains stopped passenger service. The tracks were taken up, the electricity was turned off, and most of Rhyolite's residents had abandoned the town—all but Mrs. Dyer, owner of the Mayflower Hotel, and her son, and the ghosts. The ghostly Tom Kelly is among them. Seeking his fortune, Kelly came to Rhyolite in 1905 and opened up a saloon. He ended up leaving an endearing monument to man's ingenuity—the bottle house. Using fifty thousand bottles that he'd carefully collected from saloons, Tom Kelly built his unique house at a cost of $2,500. The bottle house still stands to this day. And although Kelly never lived in the house, his ghost has been spotted in and around the house many times. Though he may appear grizzled and menacing, Tom means no harm; he simply enjoys visiting his old stomping grounds.

Over in the red-light section of the old ghost town, Mabel "Jewell" Vaughn, the first woman to buy property in Rhyolite, oversees her elegant bawdy house, and long-dead ladies of the evening still strut their stuff. Particularly noticeable is the raven-haired beauty with highly rouged cheeks who appears at all hours of the day and night. Some say she is Mona Bell, a young prostitute who was murdered on January 2, 1908, in her cottage on Main Street. The killer was her lover, Fred Skinner, and the two were involved in a violent argument. She shot at him and missed. He fired back, fatally wounding her.

Mona Bell's real name was Sarah Isabelle Peterman, and although she is buried nearly a thousand miles north in Ballard, Washington, the tragic Mona Bell is said to haunt the old red-light area of Rhyolite. The ghostly Fred Skinner, who awaited his trial in the new jail, wanders the area as well.

Rhyolite's jail contained four cells and was built in 1907 at a cost of $7,000, a lot of money in those days. There is always a jail, and apparently an inmate liked this one. He has been seen stalking the area outside the crumbling old jail building. It is odd that the ghost stays put near the jail, though. You'd think he would have put some distance between himself and captivity. But he didn't. And he appears so lifelike that tourists often mistake him for one of them.

A woman, who'd just read the rattlesnake warning sign, kindly warned the ghostly inmate of snakes as he stepped into the tall grass. But she got the surprise of her life when he glared at her and vanished in the grass. She was shaken—until she assured herself that the rattlers were more of a danger to her than any of the ghosts who might inhabit this old ghost town. And she was right, of course. Step lightly and be aware of rattlesnakes.

The Goldwell Open Air Museum, an outdoor sculpture park, is located near Rhyolite and is well worth the stop. A favorite item with ghost enthusiasts is the *Last Supper* sculpture by Belgian artist Albert Szukalski. In his life-size sculpture, Szukalski replaced the people of Leonardo da Vinci's *Last Supper* with ghostly figures. And indeed a couple of real-life ghosts are said to enjoy the sculpture so much that they often appear to visitors. But even if you don't see them, this is a unique spot for a selfie. And what self-respecting ghost enthusiast can pass that up?

The railroad tracks are long gone, as are the people who came to and from Rhyolite on the trains. And yet there are those who believe the ghost train still rolls out across the desert here. Ghost train lore is popular in many countries. Here in the United States, the most famous ghost train is that of the Lincoln funeral train that is said to run regularly from Washington, DC, to Springfield, Illinois.

The ghost train of Rhyolite may not bear the body of a beloved president, but some of those who know Rhyolite by dark will tell you that there is indeed a ghost train out here. And on those cold desert nights when the wind is fiercely blowing, the unmistakable sound of a distant train can still be heard as it makes its way toward Rhyolite.

We're about 120 miles from the glittery lights and all the excitement of Las Vegas. It's a two-hour drive, give or take. And here under some of the clearest skies in Nevada, indeed in the United States, we'll conclude our foray into Nevada's ghostly tales. I want to thank you for joining me in this adventure. If you've enjoyed delving into the ghost stories of Nevada, then I've succeeded in my quest to share the ghostly tales of Nevada, a state rich in so many things besides those that go bump in the night.

Bibliography

Books

Addenbrook, Alice B. *The Mistress of the Mansion*.

Ashbaugh, Don. *Nevada's Turbulent Yesterday: A Study of Ghost Towns*.

Beebe, Lucius, and Charles Clegg. *Legends of the Comstock Lode*.

Benson, Jackson J. *The Ox-Bow Man: A Biography of Walter Van Tilburg Clark*.

Berlin, Ellin. *Silver Platter*.

Burbank, Jeff. *True Tales of Glitter, Glamour and Greed*.

Butler, Anne M. *Daughters of Joy, Sisters of Misery: Prostitutes in the American West, 1865–90*.

Cerveri, Doris. *With Curry's Compliments: The Story of Abraham Curry*.

Clark, Walter Van Tilburg, ed. *The Journals of Alfred Doten*.

Dangberg, Grace. *Carson Valley: Historical Sketches of Nevada's First Settlement*.

Datin, Richard C. *Elegance on C Street: The Story of the International Hotel*.

Earl, Phillip. *This Was Nevada*, vol. 2.

Elliot, Russell R. *Nevada's Twentieth-Century Mining Boom: Tonopah, Goldfield, Ely*.

Ellis, Anne. *Life of an Ordinary Woman*.

Farrell, Ronald A., and Case Carole. *The Black Book and the Mob: The Untold Story of the Control of Nevada's Casinos*.

Garrison, Omar V. *Howard Hughes in Las Vegas*.

Glasscock, Carl B. *The Big Bonanza*.

Hall, Shawn R. *Romancing Nevada's Past: Ghost Towns and Historic Sites of Eureka, Lander, and White Pine Counties.*

Harpster, Jack. *100 Years in the Nevada Governor's Mansion.*

Hegne, Barbara. *Harlots, Hurdies and Spirited Women of Virginia City, Nevada.*

———. *The History of the Silver Queen Hotel.*

Hickson, Howard. *Mint Mark "CC": The Story of the United States Mint at Carson City, Nevada.*

Higgs, Gerald B. *Lost Legends of the Silver State.*

Jackson, William Turrentine. *Treasure Hill: Portrait of a Silver Mining Camp.*

James, Ronald M. *Temples of Justice.*

James, Ronald M., and Elizabeth Safford Harvey. *Nevada's Historic Buildings.*

James, Ronald M., and Susan A. James. *Castle in the Sky: George Whittell Jr. and the Thunderbird Lodge.*

James, Ronald M., and C. Elizabeth Raymond. *Comstock Women: The Making of a Mining Community.*

Kling, Dwayne. *The Rise of the Biggest Little City.*

Lewis, Oscar. *Sagebrush Casinos: The Story of Legal Gambling in Nevada.*

Loofbourow, Leon L. *Steeples among the Sage.*

McBride, Dennis. *Midnight on Arizona Street: The Secret Life of the Boulder Dam Hotel.*

McCracken, Robert D. Tonopah: *The Greatest, the Richest and the Best Mining Camp in the World.*

McDonald, Douglas. *Nevada: Lost Mines and Buried Treasures.*

Moe, Al W. *The Roots of Reno.*

Moehring, Eugene P. *Resort City in the Sunbelt: Las Vegas, 1930–1970.*

Moffat, James R. *Memoirs of an Old-Timer: A Personal Glimpse of Rhyolite, Nevada, 1906–07.*

Molinelli, Lambert. *Eureka and Its Resources.*

Murbarger, Nell. *Ghosts of the Glory Trail.*

Newton, Wayne. *Once Before I Go.*

Oberding, Janice. *Ghosts of Goldfield and Tonopah.*

———. *Haunted Lake Tahoe.*

———. *Haunted Nevada: Ghosts and Strange Phenomena of the Silver State*.

Oesterle, Joe, and Tim Cridland. *Weird Las Vegas and Nevada*.

Paher, Stanley W. *Nevada Towns and Tales*, vol. 1.

Paine, Swift. *Eilley Orrum: Queen of the Comstock*.

Patterson, Edna B., Louise A. Ulph, and Victor Goodwin. *Nevada's Northeast Frontier*.

Porter, Shirley A. *But You Can't Leave Shirley*.

Raymond, Elizabeth. *George Wingfield: Owner and Operator of Nevada*.

Reid, Ed, and Ovid Demaris. *The Green Felt Jungle*.

Riddle, Jennifer E., Sena M. Loyd, Stacy L. Branham, and Curt Thomas. *Nevada State Prison*.

Rightmire, Billie J. *Ring around the Moon*.

Roske, Ralph J. *Las Vegas: A Desert Paradise*.

Shafton, Anthony. *The Nevada They Knew: Robert Caples and Walter Van Tilburg Clark*.

Shinn, Charles Howard. *The Story of the Mine, as Illustrated by the Great Comstock Lode Nevada*.

Stevens, Joseph E. *Hoover Dam: An American Adventure*.

Stewart, Robert Ernest, Jr., and Mary Frances Stewart. *Adolph Sutro: A Biography*.

Thomas, Bob. *Liberace: The True Story*.

Townley, John M. *Tough Little Town on the Truckee*.

Twain, Mark. *Roughing It*.

Waldorf, John Taylor. *A Kid on the Comstock*.

Watson, Margaret G. *Silver Theatre Amusements of Nevada's Mining Frontier, 1850–1864*.

Weight, Harold, and Lucile Weight. *Rhyolite: The Ghost City of Golden Dreams*.

Wilkerson, William III. *The Man Who Invented Las Vegas*.

Wilson, R. Michael. *Stagecoach Robbery*.

Zanjani, Sally. *Goldfield: The Last Gold Rush on the Western Frontier*.

Newspapers

Carson Daily Appeal, February 19, 1898.

Carson Daily Appeal, May 27, 1886.
Carson Daily Appeal, November 6, 1895.
Carson Daily Appeal, September 28, 1879.
Carson Morning Appeal, May 14, 1880.
Carson Tribune, May 16, 1895.
Daily Reese River Reveille, December 13–14, 1881.
Elko Daily Independent, April 15, 1918.
Elko Daily Independent, January 29, 1892.
Elko Free Press, January 25, 1889.
Ely Daily Times, October 29, 1899.
Ely Record, December 20, 1890.
Eureka Daily Sentinel, January 29, 1882.
Eureka Daily Sentinel, March 28, 1880.
Eureka Daily Sentinel, November 5, 1875.
Eureka Daily Sentinel, September 14, 1876.
Eureka Daily Sentinel, September 5, 1876.
Gold Hill Daily News, March 31, 1873.
Gold Hill Daily News, November 25, 1872.
Great Falls Tribune, December 26, 1920.
Inyo Independent, November 30, 1872.
Las Vegas Review-Journal, February 5, 1994.
Nevada State Journal, April 5, 1906.
Pahrump Valley Times, November 4, 2016.
Reno Gazette, October 31, 1929.
Reno Gazette-Journal, January 9, 1879.
Reno Gazette-Journal, March 17, 1922.
Reno Gazette-Journal, March 18, 1990.
Territorial Enterprise, October 15, 1876.
Tonopah Bonanza, July 28, 1906.
Tonopah Daily Bonanza, September 25, 1907.

Magazines

Life, April 1949.
Premier, February 1995.

About the Author

*J*anice Oberding is a Nevada-based writer. She enjoys traveling and researching history, true crime, and the paranormal. She is one of only a few people who have spent an entire night at Alcatraz—aside from those who were incarcerated there. She worked as consultant and historian for the Alcatraz episode of SyFy's *Ghost Hunters* (with Jason Hawes and Grant Wilson).

She has also worked with the History Channel, LivingTV, and the Travel Channel and has appeared in episodes of *Dead Famous* for Twofour Productions, the Travel Channel's *Haunted Hotels* and *Ghost Adventures*, and Fox's *Scariest Places on Earth*.

Janice has previously published spooky books with Stackpole, Arcadia/History Press, Pelican Publishing, and Fonthill Publishing.

In addition to writing, she speaks at local events and paranormal conferences. Although she has had inexplicable things occur during her research, Janice remains a skeptic. You can find her online at facebook.com/JaniceOberding and @JaniceOberding on Twitter.